SWEDENBORG
OETINGER
KANT

SWEDENBORG STUDIES NO. 18

SWEDENBORG
OETINGER
KANT

THREE PERSPECTIVES
ON THE
Secrets of Heaven

Wouter J. Hanegraaff

Foreword by Inge Jonsson

Swedenborg Foundation Press
West Chester, Pennsylvania

Second printing 2013

Swedenborg Studies is a scholarly series published by the Swedenborg Foundation. The primary purpose of the series is to make materials available for understanding the life and thought of Emanuel Swedenborg (1688–1772) and the impact his thought has had on others. The Foundation undertakes to publish original studies and English translations of such studies and to republish primary sources that are otherwise difficult to access. Proposals should be sent to: Editor, Swedenborg Studies, Swedenborg Foundation, 320 North Church Street, West Chester, Pennsylvania 19380.

Credits: The Scripture quotations contained herein are from the New Revised Standard Version Bible, copyright © 1989 by the Division of Christian Education of the National Council of the Churches of Christ in the U.S.A., and are used by permission. All rights reserved.

Library of Congress Cataloging-in-Publication Data

  Swedenborg, Oetinger, Kant : three perspectives on the secrets of heaven / Wouter J. Hanegraaff.
     p. cm.—(Swedenborg studies ; no. 18)
  Includes bibliographical references and index.
  ISBN 978-0-87785-321-3
  1. Swedenborg, Emanuel, 1688-1772. Arcana coelestia. 2. Heaven—Christianity. 3. New Jerusalem Church—Doctrines. 4. Oetinger, Friedrich Christoph, 1702-1782. 5. Kant, Immanuel, 1724-1804. I. Title.

BX8712.A89H36 2007
230'.94 – dc22
2007000341

Designed by Karen Connor
Printed in the United States of America

Denn der Berg, das Korpus der Dinge, bedarf gar keines Schlüssels; nur die Nebelwand der Historie, die um ihn hängt, muss durchschritten werden. . . . Gewiss, Geschichte mag im Grunde ein Schein sein, aber ein Schein, ohne den in der Zeit keine Einsicht in das Wesen möglich ist. Im wunderlichen Hohlspiegel der philologischen Kritik kann für heutige Menschen zuerst und auf die reinlichste Weise, in den legitimen Ordnungen des Kommentars, jene mystische Totalität des Systems gesichtet werden, dessen Existenz doch grade in der Projektion auf die historische Zeit verschwindet.

Gershom Scholem
Letter to Zalman Schocken, 29 October 1937

For the mountain, the body of things, needs no key; it is only the nebulous wall of history, which hangs around it, that must be traversed. . . . True, history may at bottom be an illusion, but an illusion without which no perception of the essence is possible in time. The wondrous concave mirror of philological criticism makes it possible for the people of today first and most purely to receive a glimpse, in the legitimate orders of commentary, of that mystical totality of the system, whose existence, however, vanishes in the very act of being projected onto historical time.

❦ TABLE *of* CONTENTS ❦

❦ PART I ❦
Swedenborg's *Secrets of Heaven*

❧ PART II ❧
Oetinger, Kant, and the Early Reception of *Secrets of Heaven*

❧ FOREWORD ❧

SINCE SEPTEMBER 2006, VISITORS TO THE ROYAL SWEDISH ACADEMY OF Sciences in Stockholm are met by a plaque at the entrance telling them that one of the "Memories of the World" selected by UNESCO is preserved in the building. So far there are only two Swedish items on that list: a collection of manuscripts written by Emanuel Swedenborg (1688–1772) housed at the academy and the archives of Astrid Lindgren (1907–2002) housed at the Royal Library in Stockholm. In general, Swedes were surprised when they learned that such an ill-matched couple had been chosen by UNESCO: Lindgren, the greatest Swedish writer of children's books, whom everyone knows and loves, and a scientist and theosopher from the Age of Enlightenment, who is known by few of his compatriots and read by even fewer, in spite of the fact that Ralph Waldo Emerson selected him to be one of his "Representative Men" and other proofs of his international fame.

Being a bachelor, Emanuel Swedenborg had no direct heirs. His distant relatives donated a chest with more than 20,000 manuscript pages to the Royal Academy of Sciences in December 1772, eight months after his death. Swedenborg had become a member of the academy a year after its foundation in 1739, so it was natural for his relatives to hand over the literary property he left to this prestigious institution. A decade later, however, they regretted the decision after they had received a generous offer to sell the collection to England, as had been done with the manuscripts of Swedenborg's famous relative Carl Linnaeus. The Royal Academy succeeded in defending its right to the Swedenborg papers against this attack, and again against a second one in the 1820s. Unfortunately, the academy did not take particularly good care of the donation for quite some time. It took almost twenty years before the collection was passably registered, and the permanent secretaries lent manuscripts rather irresponsibly to Swedenborg's early followers. Some of these loans were adrift abroad for decades. Not until the beginning of the twentieth century did the Academy publish any of the manuscripts; and even that project was closed down after the third volume. Nowadays, however, the collection is restored to its original condition. It is safely preserved in a modern archive building, and a program of updating the catalogue is underway.

What was UNESCO's primary motivation for selecting Swedenborg's manuscripts out of hundreds of other candidates to the "Memories of the World" list? The main reason is that Emanuel Swedenborg was a unique person, who devoted the last quarter of his life to interpreting the Bible after a laudable career as scientist and mining engineer. The reports of otherworld experiences and conversations with angels and spirits, which he published in works such as *De Coelo et Ejus Mirabilibus, et de Inferno* (*Heaven and Hell*, 1758) and *De Telluribus in Mundo Nostro Solari* (*Other Planets*, also 1758) and also inserted in the theosophic writings from *Arcana Coelestia* (*Secrets of Heaven*, published between 1749 and 1756) to *Vera christiana religio* (*True Christianity*, published in 1771), made him renowned— and notorious—during his lifetime. The road that ended in the divine call to reveal the secrets of heaven certainly passed along paths that were well-known and highly respected by contemporary scientists; but with the wisdom of hindsight, it is easy to discern several signs that portended sublime ambitions to reach a loftier goal than making scientific discoveries or building philosophical systems.

A short restatement of Swedenborg's biography might be of some use as an introduction to Wouter Hanegraaff's elucidative presentation of how this goal was achieved and what consequences it had in contemporary Germany. After he completed his studies at Uppsala University in 1709, Emanuel Swedberg, as he was called before he was ennobled ten years later, set out on his first journey abroad. For almost five years, he traveled to England, the Netherlands, France, and Germany. As a student, he had been devoted to mathematics and science, and during his journey, he visited many well-known scholars and scientists in those fields. His idol in Sweden was Christopher Polhem (1661–1751), a self-taught inventor; and after coming back from his journey, Swedenborg published a journal, the very name of which paid tribute to Polhem: *Daedalus hyperboreus* (The Northern Inventor, 1716–1718). Its main purpose was to publish descriptions of quite a few ingenious inventions made by Polhem; but in this first scientific journal in Sweden, young Swedberg also printed articles of his own on various problems in science and technology. King Charles XII read a copy of the journal in his headquarters in Lund and called for the editor. Their meeting went so well that the king appointed Swedberg assessor of the College of Mines, with a special commission to serve as assistant to Polhem.

Swedenborg cooperated with Polhem for some years, but after the autocratic king had fallen in November 1718, the College of Mines refused to accept his appointment for a long period of time. To improve his qualifications, Swedenborg set out on his second journey abroad in 1721–1722—among other reasons, to study mining in the Harzgebirge—and he published two considerable volumes on mineralogical and philosophical topics during the journey. In 1724, he was commissioned by the College of Mines to evaluate the potential utility of a steam engine in mining. This was the first technological assessment in Sweden, and Swedenborg's recommendations were accepted without reservation. During the next ten years, Swedenborg was fully engaged in his official duties, as well as in his private business activities, and he did not publish anything. However, during his third journey abroad, it became clear that he had collected a great amount of data in this decade of silence. Three impressive folios were printed in Dresden and Leipzig in 1734 with the common name of *Opera philosophica et mineralia*. Two of them were about the production of copper and iron, and they strengthened his already high reputation as a mining expert.

For his personal development, however, the philosophical volume turned out to be the most important of the three. *Principia rerum naturalium*, as it is usually called for short, or "First Principles of Natural Things, or New Attempts to Explain Philosophically the Primordial World," contains exactly what its exhaustive title promises. Here Swedenborg presented a theory of the birth of inorganic nature out of the mathematical point and of its development up to our planetary system, based mainly on modified Cartesian ideas. The book bears witness to his wide reading in ancient as well as modern philosophy of nature, and an admirable capacity for carrying out a grandiose vision consistently. It also contains one of Swedenborg's weightiest contributions to science, namely, his modification of Descartes's theory of the planetary system. Instead of the planets being attracted to the sun, Swedenborg conceived that, in the beginning, enormous masses of matter had been hurled out of the sun; and after cooling, they gradually developed into planets and positioned themselves in their respective orbits. His idea may be seen as a precursor of the Kant–Laplace nebular hypothesis, and it has been suggested that he may even have inspired that hypothesis via Buffon, who had a copy of *Principia rerum naturalium* in his library.

But this is only a hypothesis. For Swedenborg himself, the book concluded his mostly mechanistic philosophy of nature. In the same year as *Opera philosophica et mineralia*, he published a booklet with two essays, one about the concept of infinity and the other about the interaction between the soul and the body: it is usually called *De Infinito*. In the second essay, he presented a program for his future research, which was one of the most audacious in the history of science. The goal was to find empirical evidence for the immortality of the soul: *ut ipsis sensibus demonstretur animae immortalitas*. During a leave of absence from his official duties in 1736—which actually lasted four years and was spent in France, Italy, and the Netherlands—Swedenborg studied with almost unimaginable energy human anatomy and physiology on the hunt for the seat of the soul. His hard work resulted in six large volumes, all written in Latin as almost every one of his published works, and a great number of manuscripts, of which his notes on the human brain continue to be admired by and of interest to twenty-first-century scientists. Posthumously published excerpts of his notebooks show how Swedenborg also consulted an elite of ancient and modern philosophers—Plato, Aristotle, Augustine, Malebranche, Leibniz, Wolff, and others—in his efforts to provide a theoretical foundation for his views of the intercommunication of the soul with the senses and through them with the world of matter.

Of course, such an imaginative research program could not be carried out. In the spring of 1745, Swedenborg was released from the impossible task he had imposed on himself by a divine call to reform Christianity. This happened at the end of his fifth journey abroad. He had made notes during all his previous travels, and he did so even now, but this time the diary, known as his *Journal of Dreams*, contains little data on people he met and on his work. Instead it reflects a deep mental crisis, which was partly provoked by the struggle for more powerful means of expression than the language of science. During the years preceding the crisis, Swedenborg had formulated a doctrine of forms, a second on series and degrees, and a third on correspondences and representations; and he tried to use them all in attempting to create a poetic synthesis of his philosophical and scientific views, which was written immediately after the crisis, *De cultu et amore Dei* (*Worship and Love of God*). But the goal was still not within reach, and the book remained uncompleted. He had to find firm ground first, and he did finally in the Divine Word, the original purity and truth of which he was now called to restore.

After his return to Sweden in 1745, Swedenborg went back to work in the College of Mines and at the same time started extensive studies of the Old Testament, the immediate result of which was a commentary on the story of creation in Genesis. Two years later he resigned his governmental position and again traveled abroad to complete and publish his first exegetical volumes. With this decisive move, he concluded his career as scientist and technician and started his literary activities, which were to make him world famous but also expose him to scorn and contempt. One of the numerous New Church commentators, who have complained that Emanuel Swedenborg has been disregarded by historians of science, found a simple explanation "in the fact that [Swedenborg] wrote the *Arcana Coelestia.*" The commentator is probably right, although there are other factors that have contributed to the silence of historians. Swedenborg did not hold a university chair, and thus he had no students. Few discoveries are attached to his name, and his probably most important achievements—his studies of the human brain—lay hidden in manuscripts for more than a century.

Regardless of how they are evaluated, Swedenborg's experiences as a scientist had a decisive effect on his ideas of the spiritual world. The all-embracing vision of the societies of spirits as parts of a universal human body, a *Maximus Homo*, is based on his profound knowledge of anatomy and physiology. In his *memorabilia*, debates often take place that recall public defences of academic theses, and the argumentation exhibits the rationalism of the Age of Enlightenment. As Wouter Hanegraaff elaborates in his convincing analysis, Swedenborg belongs to the same tradition of rationalism from Leibniz and Wolff as Kant, which probably accounts for the unusual malice and the occasionally vulgar mockery in *Träume eines Geistersehers*. Kant's acrid criticism may be explained not only by his disappointment after reading Swedenborg's books, for which he had paid a lot of money, but also by his own need to hold his metaphysical urge in check.

The credit for the UNESCO's recognition of Swedenborg should be given first to his devoted followers. Thanks to New Church societies and foundations in Great Britain, the United States, and Switzerland, Swedenborg's published books have been translated and most of his manuscripts printed, so that his message can be heard and discussed all over the world.

The body of Swedenborg literature is still dominated by New Church commentators, who have made many valuable contributions; but there can be no doubt that the historical position of this remarkable man and his writings would benefit from being analyzed also by many more non-confessional scholars. Not only neutral historians of science, who have left Swedenborg out of their accounts, but also theologians and exegetes to a great extent have neglected his work. Therefore, it is a real pleasure to note that a prominent scholar of such international standing as Wouter Hanegraaff has found Swedenborg interesting enough to study. The results are much more instructive and inspiring than "a modest exercise in clarification by means of complexification," as he has promised to deliver in his introduction. Dr. Hanegraaff's valuable book proves beyond doubt that UNESCO had very good reasons for making Swedenborg's manuscripts a "memory of the world."

Inge Jonsson
Stockholm 2007

❈ ACKNOWLEDGMENTS ❈

I would like to thank the Swedenborg Foundation for inviting the research project that eventually led to both my introduction to the "New Century Edition" of Swedenborg's *Secrets of Heaven* and the greatly expanded and re-edited version that is hereby published in book form. In particular, I would like to thank (in alphabetical order) Mary Lou Bertucci, Deborah Forman, Jonathan Rose, and Stuart Shotwell. For reading and commenting upon earlier versions of the text, or parts of it, I would like to thank Jean-Pierre Brach, Antoine Faivre, Gregory Johnson, Inge Jonsson, Bernd Roling, Friedemann Stengel, Jane Williams-Hogan, and my students at the University of Amsterdam.

❦ INTRODUCTION ❧

IN 1749, EMANUEL SWEDENBORG (1688–1772) PUBLISHED THE FIRST VOLUME of what would become the foundational work of his visionary period. The full title given in the first of the eight volumes (other volume titles vary slightly) is *Arcana Coelestia, Quae in Scriptura Sacra, seu Verbo Domini Sunt, Detecta: Hic Primum Quae in Genesis: Una cum Mirabilibus Quae Visa Sunt in Mundo Spirituum, et in Coelo Angelorum* (A Disclosure of Secrets of Heaven Contained in Sacred Scripture, or the Word of the Lord, Beginning with Those in Genesis: Together with Wonders Seen in the World of Spirits and in the Heaven of Angels). For two hundred years it has been known simply as *Arcana Coelestia* (Secrets of Heaven) or, among Swedenborg's followers, as the *Arcana*. Ostensibly the work interprets the meaning of Genesis and Exodus; but, in fact, it is much more than just an exegesis, as it includes accounts of Swedenborg's spiritual experiences and some extended doctrinal tracts.

The *Arcana*, to which I will henceforth refer as *Secrets of Heaven*, has obviously been of major importance to Swedenborg's followers since the eighteenth century and up to the present, since it contains the doctrinal, exegetical, and visionary foundations of his highly innovative theological vision. But beyond its significance for Swedenborgians, the work is extremely interesting as a focal point for studying the complex interactions during the later eighteenth century between traditional Christian theology, the new types of Enlightenment rationality and science, and a variety of "hermetic" or "esoteric" attempts at finding a middle ground between those two extremes.[1] With the publication of *Secrets of Heaven*, Swedenborg established himself as a major player in this third category, and thereby provoked strong reactions from all sides. The important Württemberg theosopher and theologian Friedrich Christoph Oetinger (1702–1782) was likewise looking for a middle ground and thought at first that he had found a kindred spirit in Swedenborg; however, he eventually discovered—to his dismay, as will be seen—that Swedenborg's perspective and his own were wholly antithetical. Thus, the story of Oetinger's reception of Swedenborg's *Secrets of Heaven* demonstrates how much room for diversity and conflict there was among those who agreed about the need for a "third way" between traditional orthodoxy and scientific rationality.

Immanuel Kant (1724–1804), of course, was not looking for such a middle ground but represents the rationalist perspective. By studying his reactions to Swedenborg, we discover how and why the work of a "spirit seer" could become a major intellectual challenge to one of the greatest thinkers of the Enlightenment. For contrary to what has been assumed by almost all Kant specialists, even up to the present day,[2] Kant did not take Swedenborg's metaphysics lightly or dismiss it out of hand as an "occult" chimera; although the mocking and ironic tone of his treatise on Swedenborg, *Dreams of a Spirit Seer*, was remarkably successful in diverting attention away from the fact, *Secrets of Heaven* actually presented Kant with very serious philosophical problems. The solutions he found for them in this fascinating text—the last of Kant's "pre-critical" writings—set him on a course, as will be seen, that would eventually lead to his mature critical philosophy.

In short, Swedenborg and his two most important early critics are emblematic of major ideological positions in the eighteenth-century conflict between religion and reason: Swedenborg and Oetinger represent two different, conflicting options within the domain of "Enlightenment esotericism," whereas Kant represents the secular rationalist perspective. These three are, without any doubt, by far the most important figures in the early critical debate about *Secrets of Heaven*, and hence they are the central figures in this book. However, among the various minor figures that played a role in that debate, some special attention will also be given to authors such as Johann August Ernesti (1707–1781), an early representative of the third theoretical position, that of Christian orthodoxy. Thus, all three major theoretical perspectives are represented in the discussions that follow. Together they provide often surprising insights into the issues that were at stake when scientists, philosophers, theologians, and esotericists during the Age of Reason attempted to conceive of a heavenly reality and relate it to scientific and rational discourse.

Before we get to *Secrets of Heaven* itself, it is important to address a central but traditionally sensitive issue in Swedenborg scholarship: the problem of his sources. Broadly speaking, three opinions can be distinguished here. First, according to what might be called an "orthodox" Swedenborgian perspective, Swedenborg's insights have their source directly in heaven.

Since it was the Lord[3] himself who disclosed to him the secrets of heaven as well as the true meaning of the biblical Scriptures, Swedenborg was obviously not dependent on any mundane traditions or sources, whether religious, philosophical, or scientific. From this perspective, any attempt at understanding Swedenborg by means of historical contextualization and the critical study of sources is not only futile, but fundamentally misguided.

Second, according to a more moderate, "providentialist" variant of the orthodox perspective, the Lord's guidance was already discreetly at work during Swedenborg's scientific career. His passionate search for rational understanding, concerned with problems such as the interaction between soul and body, can be seen in hindsight as a necessary preparation for his visionary career: Swedenborg first needed to push strict scientific inquiry as far as he could and discover for himself the inherent limitations of reason before he was ready for the Lord to provide him with the direct visionary insight that science could never give. From this perspective, the study of mundane sources may not be decisive but is legitimate and interesting; at the very least, it provides us with edifying illustrations of the Lord's providential designs.

From a third perspective, that of the historian, it is simply impossible to either prove or disprove the believer's claim that Swedenborg's insights were inspired by heaven. The historian of religions and religious ideas is bound to a stance of "methodological agnosticism" regarding the existence or non-existence of heaven.[4] From this perspective, it becomes critically important to investigate what sources and traditions may have influenced Swedenborg's thinking and to ask whether such influences might help us understand—and even "explain," at least partially—the nature and foundations of his mature worldview. Still, even in instances where such research suggests that Swedenborg strongly depended on previous sources and traditions, it can never be conclusively demonstrated, in any strict scientific sense, that he was *not* inspired by heaven: "providential" interpretations may be superfluous and hence irrelevant to the historian, but theoretically they always remain possible.

Since the author of this book is not a Swedenborgian, and therefore cannot approach Swedenborg's *Secrets of Heaven* from either the first or the second perspective, the following analysis will be informed by a historical-contextual approach, based upon a stance of "agnostic" neutrality regarding the ultimate source of Swedenborg's insights. Among previous scholars who have taken a similar approach, we can distinguish between two main lines of interpretation concerning Swedenborg's sources. Major biographers such as Martin Lamm (1880–1950) (Lamm [1915] 2000) and Inge Jonsson (Jonsson 1970; Jonsson 1979; Jonsson [1971] 1999) have strongly emphasized the continuity between Swedenborg's scientific and visionary phase: as formulated by Jonsson, "In order to explain rationally his continuous experiences with spirits and angels during and after the great spiritual crisis around the middle of the 1740s, Swedenborg needed to make only small changes in his psycho-physical theorizing, mainly simplifications."[5] Thus, Swedenborg's scientific and philosophical worldview—based upon broadly Cartesian foundations and strongly influenced by rationalist thinkers such as Gottfried Wilhelm Leibniz (1646–1716), Christian Wolff (1679–1754), and Nicolas de Malebranche (1638–1715)—is of decisive importance for understanding his mature theosophy; although the latter may at first sight look like a sharp break with the scientific theorizing of the past, it is actually a spiritual reformulation of it.

Other Swedenborg specialists, such as, for example, Ernst Benz (1907–1978) (Benz [1969] 2000) and Marsha Keith Schuchard (Schuchard 1995; Schuchard 1998; Schuchard 1999; Schuchard 2001), while not denying the relevance of Swedenborg's scientific background, suggest that the essential sources of his spiritual worldview lie elsewhere. Swedenborg is presented by them as a modern representative of Western esotericism,[6] whose worldview is ultimately based upon such currents as Neoplatonism, the Hermetic philosophy of the Renaissance, Jewish and Christian Kabbalah, and the Christian theosophy of Jacob Böhme (1575–1624) and his followers.

One obvious problem with this second interpretation is the paucity of explicit references on Swedenborg's part to Western esoteric authors and traditions;[7] but authors in favor of an "esoteric Swedenborg" tend to explain this fact by suggesting that he must have intentionally suppressed them because he feared that quotations from Kabbalists and mystics might discredit his work in the eyes of his rationalist readers. In the absence of many explicit source references, the alleged dependence of Swedenborg's worldview on traditional esoteric cosmologies is defended by invoking the structural similarity that is claimed to exist between them. Unfortunately, however, if one studies these comparisons, one finds that they tend to be quite superficial, certainly if compared with the detailed critical discussions by authors such as Jonsson, who argue in favor of Swedenborg's dependence on rationalist and scientific models and concepts. Although the present author began his research in the expectation of finding significant debts on Swedenborg's part to Western esoteric traditions, close study of *Secrets of Heaven* and other works, as well as of the relevant secondary literature, has convinced him that the "exoteric" Swedenborg defended by Lamm and Jonsson is much closer to the truth than the "esoteric" one.[8]

This is not to deny, however, that Swedenborg was aware of a range of philosophers of nature influenced by hermetic, alchemical, and Kabbalistic traditions. His library catalog shows that he owned books of this kind; he must have had some familiarity with the outlines of Jacob Böhme's system (although mostly indirectly, by mediation of Johann Konrad Dippel [1678–1734]);[9] he sometimes uses terminology derived from the Paracelsian tradition; and he was certainly familiar with the Cambridge Platonists Henry More (1614–1687) and Ralph Cudworth (1617–1688) as well as with the Christian Kabbalist Franciscus Mercurius van Helmont (1614–1698). In addition, he was seriously influenced by the "divine physics" of his contemporary Andreas Rüdiger (1673–1731). However, we should realize that it was quite normal for an erudite scientist and natural philosopher in the first half of the eighteenth century to be acquainted with such authors and their ideas, since they were still very much a normal part of acceptable philosophical and scientific discourse; in fact, it would have been strange if Swedenborg had *not* been aware of them. Generally, however, he seems to have been interested in their more strictly philosophical insights concerning the workings of nature and its relation to the soul. The influence of the authors just mentioned does not add up to an "esoteric philosophy" in the sense of an integrated religious worldview based upon hermetic, alchemical, or Kabbalistic foundations and referring to supra-rational sources of revelation (*gnosis*); nor is there evidence that Swedenborg believed in a "perennial philosophy" passed on and kept alive by divinely inspired teachers through the ages.[10]

Indeed, Swedenborg seems to belong to the select group of true innovators in the history of Western religion: rather than as a link in a chain of esoteric authors from antiquity to modern times, he must be seen as the founder of a new type of Christianity that eventually became of fundamental importance not only for the small church groups that developed directly from it but for various new kinds of Western esotericism as well. That Swedenborg's work has become of extremely great importance to Western esoteric currents since the eighteenth century is not in any doubt; but since later esotericists often combined authentic Swedenborgian concepts with ideas that are alien to his worldview, one might say that this is the case in spite of Swedenborg's intentions rather than because of them.[11]

Against these backgrounds, it seems appropriate to end with a remark of more general applicability. Instead of attempting to situate Swedenborg within—and hence confine him to—one specific "tradition" or another (whether esoteric, Christian, philosophical or scientific), it makes more sense to see him as participating simultaneously in a series of overlapping and competing discourses.[12] And in fact, a similar shift of perspective is equally useful with respect to our two other main protagonists and to the relation between them. Oetinger has often been presented as one of the main representatives of a Western esoteric tradition known as Christian Theosophy, and of another one known as Christian Kabbalah;[13] but as will become clear from our discussions, there is as much reason to see him as a remarkably orthodox representative of biblical fundamentalism as understood in the Protestant tradition. Far from being contradictory, such a combination reflects the complexity that might be expected from a thinker who actively participated in the various discourses that were competing with one another in his lifetime and society.

Finally, a similar argument may be applied even to Immanuel Kant: his uncontested centrality to the history of philosophy and to the philosophy of the Enlightenment, in particular, does not detract from the fact that he was also happy to participate in various other discourses, for example, those that dealt with astronomy, psychiatry,[14] or—as in our case—the possibilities of contact with spirits and angels. Again, by studying those dimensions of Kant's work and integrating the results with what we already knew (or thought we knew), we gain a better perspective on the complexity of his oeuvre.

Underlying the argument of this book as a whole, then, is a broader historiographical agenda of moving away from simple black-and-white oppositions of "religion versus reason" and their various analogues (such as "Enlightenment" versus "the occult") as applied to the eighteenth century. As will be seen, such perspectives fail to do justice not only to "esoteric" authors such as Swedenborg and Oetinger, but even to icons of rationality such as Kant. Enlightenment thinkers—and here Swedenborg must certainly be included in that category—were concerned with drawing clear and sharp distinctions between reason and unreason, truth and error: they simply did not like the ambiguity of "gray areas" or shadow zones between light and darkness. Unfortunately for them, such a quest for clarity and simplicity, laudable though it might be, leads to distortions if it is applied to the notoriously messy realities described by critical historiography: history just happens to consist of "tones of gray," and its patterns tend to become more complex the closer one looks at the sources.

The book that follows, then, may be understood as a modest exercise in clarification by means of complexification, and perhaps even of edification by means of deconstruction. Such a project may sound paradoxical to some; but if history holds any secrets—as suggested by Gershom Scholem in the opening quotation—it is only by such a road that they might be disclosed.

SWEDENBORG
OETINGER
KANT

PART ONE

Swedenborg's *Secrets of Heaven*

1

A Key to the Secrets:
Swedenborg's Doctrine of Correspondences

To understand Swedenborg's *Secrets of Heaven*, we first need to look at the nature of his famous "doctrine of correspondences." And it is highly significant, as will be seen, that this doctrine is first presented not in a revelatory work but in one of the last products of his "scientific period." In 1741 or 1742, shortly before the religious crisis that would transform him from a scientist into a visionary, Swedenborg wrote a short and technical philosophical work entitled *A Hieroglyphic Key to Natural and Spiritual Arcana by Way of Representations and Correspondences*.[15] Seven years later appeared the first volume of what was to be his first and largest visionary work: the *Arcana Coelestia*. As the very titles indicate, both publications are explicitly devoted to *arcana* or secrets; but whereas the earlier work discusses the correspondences between natural and spiritual secrets, the later one purportedly concentrates on "heavenly" secrets only. Nevertheless, at closer examination, the earlier work turns out to be precisely what the title would seem to promise: it is in fact a major "key" to understanding Swedenborg's *Secrets of Heaven* and illustrates the remarkable continuity between one of his last scientific/philosophical works and his first visionary one.

The *Hieroglyphic Key* deals not with a "mystical" doctrine based upon supra-rational revelatory insights, but is a product of straightforward rationalist argumentation, ultimately based upon mathematics.[16] Highly trained in contemporary philosophy and mechanical science, and acutely aware of their implications, Swedenborg saw himself faced with the specter of materialist reductionism: did intellectual honesty and respect for inescapable facts require him to dismiss traditional concepts of the soul and of a supreme divine reality as mere pious illusions, since everything that had once been attributed to God and the soul could now be reduced to the workings of blind mechanical forces and material realities? As a Christian, Swedenborg found this option unacceptable. Should we, then, simply close our eyes to the evidence of science and refuse to listen to the arguments of reason, in a blind and irrational "leap of faith"? Should we perhaps seek to sideline science altogether by adopting a Platonist or Neoplatonist idealist perspective, insisting that the material realities studied by science are ultimately just illusory shadows of the divine ideas, which alone are "real"? For the scientist Swedenborg, these were no solutions at all: by beating a retreat along such escape routes, one in fact admits intellectual defeat. In short, reducing the "higher" realities of God and the soul to the "lower" reality of matter was no less unacceptable to Swedenborg than the alternative of reducing the "lower" realities (studied by science) to the status of mere shadows of the "higher" ones. How to escape from this dilemma?

Any reader who, allured by the esoteric-sounding title, opens Swedenborg's *Hieroglyphic Key* in the expectation of being introduced to realms of mystery and the occult is bound to be sobered by the dry formalism of the first sentences: "As long as motion endures so long does *conatus* endure; for *conatus* is the motive force of nature. But *conatus* alone is a dead force" (*Hieroglyphic Key* §1). This is a general statement about physical nature: nature has a motive force, technically referred to as *conatus*, that causes motion. Swedenborg continues with a second sentence of identical structure, which states that what is true on the level of physical nature has its exact correspondence on the level of psychology: the human mind also has a driving force, referred to as the will, and this force causes action. He concludes with a third sentence: on the theological level as well, there is something that corresponds precisely with the levels of nature and the mind, namely, divine providence, which is at the root of God's divine operation. Thus, we end up with a simple picture based upon the idea of three corresponding "levels of meaning":

God	Providence	→	Divine operation
Humanity	Will	→	Action
Nature	*Conatus*	→	Motion

In the rest of the *Hieroglyphic Key*, Swedenborg systematically develops this idea by giving twenty further examples of how constellations of concepts pertaining to the material world correspond with constellations of concepts pertaining to humankind and to the divine. Almost every example consists of a similar set of three corresponding short propositions, followed by a longer explanation of what the propositions mean, a set of arguments to confirm the truth of the propositions, and finally a set of general "rules" that can be inferred from them. For instance, example III states that, on the physical level, there is no motion without *conatus* but conversely there can be *conatus* without motion; this is because, if each and every *conatus* were to "break out into open motion, the world would perish, since there would be no equilibrium" (*Hieroglyphic Key* §10). Likewise, on the psychological level, there is no action without will, but conversely there is will without action: humanity would not be able to survive if there were not many "checks and resistencies" (*Hieroglyphic Key* §11) that keep us from acting out every single impulse of the will, thus causing us to moderate our actions. And likewise, on the level of the divine, there is no divine operation without providence, but conversely some providence is "not operative or effective": although God "provided and willed that all men should be saved," if his providence were invariably to take effect, it would mean that humanity's free will would be overruled. Since free will is essential to morality, there are indeed "those who resist the Divine grace; and upon such men this providence cannot be effective and operative" (*Hieroglyphic Key* §12).

Anybody familiar with Swedenborg's mature religious vision will recognize here one of his fundamental ideas; and in several other places, the *Hieroglyphic Key* contains clear prefigurations of his mature spiritual worldview.[17] The significant fact is that such ideas are here presented as logical inferences within a pre-revelatory work of technical rationalist philosophy. To understand how the latter laid the foundations for *Secrets of Heaven*, we need to take a closer look at the basic theory.

The all-important thing to note is that none of the three levels can or should be "reduced" to any other. It would not be correct to understand Swedenborg as saying that what is known as providence on the divine level somehow manifests as will on the human level (that is to say, that providence is the hidden essence of the will) or that the natural force of *conatus* manifests as providence on the divine level (that is to say, that what looks like providence is really a form of *conatus*), and so on.

To explain Swedenborg's actual meaning, it may be useful to invoke an example taken from the domain of music. A physicist from another planet who taps into an earthly music hall might make a recording of a Brahms symphony and, in order to report back to his or her people, produce a complete and accurate description of its physical qualities. Every single sound, up to the tiniest nuance, can be reduced to exact patterns of physical frequencies and graphically represented on frequency charts. As far as strictly physical realities are concerned, nothing about the symphony will be missing in such a representation, which can give a complete description of it. But, of course, from the perspective of human listeners, it is anything but complete—in fact, these patterns and charts are wholly irrelevant to them. Listeners do not hear or care about ordered frequency patterns; they are listening to music. To them, the music contains a message that the interplanetary scientist cannot possibly deduce from his charts, and that message carries an emotional content which his equipment cannot pick up. Some members of the earthly audience may be musicologists: in addition to enjoying the music, they are also trained to analyze it, and they will be aware of multiple patterns and connections that are not consciously recognized by the other listeners and can be only indirectly inferred by the interplanetary scientist.[18]

Finally, we happen to know that Johannes Brahms (1833–1897) himself believed he was directly inspired by God, who used him as a "channel" for divine revelation: "straightaway the ideas flow in upon me, directly from God."[19] Some listeners may accept Brahms's belief and perceive his music as a divine revelation, a message to humanity in a form perceptible to humankind; others may be more skeptical and hold that Brahms was mistaken in thinking that his music flowed into his mind from a divine source. While the former have no means of proving the divinity of Brahms's message to the skeptics, the latter have no means of disproving it either. But what can be said is that, according to some listeners at least, the symphony has a religious or *divine* level of meaning in addition to the *human* and the *physical* ones:

I	God's message	Divine
II	Brahms's symphony	Human
III	Frequency charts	Physical

Now the question is: to what extent can we learn something about one level by studying another?

To begin at the lowest level, studying the scientist's frequency charts does not get us even one step closer to understanding the higher levels of either the symphony or its divine original. It is true that, without the frequencies, there would be no music, just as without physical bodies there is no humanity; but the fact that humanity has a physical substratum does not mean that knowledge of the physical level teaches us anything relevant to the human one. Our knowledge of the frequencies is relevant to physicists but wholly irrelevant to listeners or musicologists.

Second, at the intermediate level of listening to the symphony (or of studying it as musicologists), we again fail to approach even one step closer to the lowest level—that of the frequencies (but neither is there any reason that we should, since we have just seen that such knowledge is irrelevant to the listener).

But might listening to the middle level of the music get us closer to understanding the highest level, that is to say, the divine message? Here—for the first and, as will be seen, the only time—the answer is positive. But while it is true that the (musical) medium is meant to convey a (divine) message, obviously it is not true that the medium *is* the message.

Before returning to this crucial point below, we must complete our inquiry into the possibilities of inter-level translation by asking ourselves whether studying the highest, divine level might teach us something about the lower ones. Again, the answer is negative: just as listening to music does not teach us anything about the lower level of frequencies, likewise we cannot assume that direct access to God's mind would teach us something about the intermediate level of music (let alone about the even lower one of frequencies). Divine revelation teaches us about the divine; it does not consist of information about "outward" humanity or material realities.

Our example of a symphony allows us to draw three conclusions, all of which are highly relevant to understanding Swedenborg's doctrine of correspondences. First, while studying "human" realities may teach us something about the divine, studying physical realities does not contribute anything to our understanding of either human realities or divine ones. What we learn from studying physics is relevant to physics only; by studying nature we learn about nature and nothing more. This insight helps explain why Swedenborg entirely dropped the study of physical science once he had developed his doctrine of correspondences.[20] His worldview contained *three* fundamental levels—natural (that is, physical, material), human, and divine—but while he still discussed all three of them in the *Hieroglyphic Key*, he chose to ignore the physical level once he had convinced himself that science in and of itself cannot teach us anything about the soul or God (that is, humanity and the divine). As a result, scientific discussions no longer play a leading role in *Secrets of Heaven* and the rest of his revelatory works. Swedenborg henceforth concentrates on only two of the three levels, now referred to as external and internal, or this world and the other one. Henceforth, when Swedenborg speaks of the external world, he actually means the human life-world.

Second, the musical example illustrates how we can have one phenomenon (a symphony) with three levels of meaning (physical, human, divine), which correspond to one another but cannot be reduced to one another. A specific melody clearly corresponds directly with a specific pattern of frequencies (and, one imagines, with a certain strand of thought in God's message); but suggesting that we discover the real meaning of the melody by printing out the frequency graph is no less absurd than suggesting that we discover the real meaning of the frequency graph by playing the melody. Each of the three levels is discrete and has its own autonomous reality, none of the three can replace any other, and none can be reduced to any other. Hence, Swedenborg can write in his *Hieroglyphic Key* that

> the principal matter must be expressed not by identical terms, but by different terms proper to each class . . . and, in fact, by terms which at first sight do not seem to signify or represent the same thing. For it is not at once comprehended that will corresponds to conatus, and providence to will; or that the rational mind corresponds to nature, and God to the rational mind. (*Hieroglyphic Key* §4 [rules 2–3])

Terms like will and *conatus* "signify or represent the same thing"—that is to say, providence—not in the sense that they actually mean the same thing as providence (for that is precisely the point: providence is providence only on its own proper level, the divine), but that will on the human level and *conatus* on the physical level *correspond* to what is providence on the divine level. In other words, none of the three can be reduced to any other.

Third, the musical example shows that there is something unique about the intermediate or human level: it is the only one that can be studied in order to discover something about *another* level. Studying frequency charts does not teach us anything about either music or the divine message it intends to convey; and direct access to God's mind does not teach us anything about his musical message or about physical frequencies. By studying physics, we learn about physics; by studying the divine, we learn about the divine. By studying the intermediate human level, however, we can by means of analogy learn something about the highest level, that of the divine, as well. And this, I suggest, provides us with another key to understanding *Secrets of Heaven*. As will be explained in more detail below, this work is explicitly based upon Swedenborg's direct visionary experiences, on the one hand, and his biblical exegesis, on the other. In other words, he claims that we may learn about the divine in two ways: first, by direct contact with it, a privileged way of knowledge that, at least at present, is considered to be hardly available to others than Swedenborg himself (through "things heard and seen," as Swedenborg called it; see most famously *Heaven and Hell* §1 and the full title of that work); and second, by interpreting God's message to humanity, the Bible. Again, the doctrine of correspondences as explained in the *Hieroglyphic Key* provided Swedenborg with a theoretical basis and justification for his project, since it states that the meaning of a term on the human level may be very different from its meaning on the higher level of the divine. On that basis, it can be assumed that the "outer meaning" of biblical terms and expressions corresponds with an "inner meaning" that may not be immediately apparent, or not apparent at all. If so, it becomes critically important to decode the Bible, and unveil the *arcana* hidden in it. The key that breaks the code, however, cannot be found in the Bible itself but has to be revealed by direct contact with the highest level (just as it requires divine grace to hear the divine message present in the symphony).

It was emphasized above that Swedenborg was searching for an alternative to both material reductionism and "(Neo)platonic" idealism, the first of which would reduce the higher to the lower, whereas the second would reduce the lower to the higher. The doctrine of correspondences developed in the *Hieroglyphic Key* went a long way towards formulating such an alternative, but it could not entirely solve the dilemma. Even though the human and material levels are discrete and autonomous, the relation in terms of ontological status between the divine, the human, and the physical realms still needed to be explained. That Swedenborg finally came to assume—somewhat ambiguously and half-heartedly—a clear-cut ontological hierarchy among the three levels of reality, along broadly (Neo)platonic lines, is evident from the final paragraph of the *Hieroglyphic Key*: "Exemplars are in the spiritual world; images and types are in the soul's kingdom;[21] but simulacra in nature" (*Hieroglyphic Key* §67 [rule 1]). The status of physical nature as a domain that contains merely simulacra further helps explain why—reluctantly and after much inner struggle, for his heart was with science—Swedenborg chose largely to ignore it in his subsequent writings. We are left, then, with a broadly Platonic distinction between the spiritual world that contains "exemplars" and a human world of autonomous but secondary status, which contains images and types reflecting the exemplars.

In an earlier analysis, I argued that Swedenborg's doctrine of correspondences was attractive to him

> *not* because it unites mind and nature, but for precisely the *contrary* reason: because it solved (for him) the Cartesian dilemma. It enabled him to retain a fundamental distinction between spirit and nature (modeled upon the distinction between *res cogitans* and *res extensa*); to continue seeing spirit as the active cause and nature as the passive substance "acted upon" by spirit; but to explain that relationship without having to assume the existence of mechanisms of instrumental causality. (Hanegraaff 1996–1998, 428)

I still maintain that this analysis is correct as far as Swedenborg's original scientific project is concerned, that is to say, the project of clarifying the relation between soul and body. The *Hieroglyphic Key* essentially contains his solution to this problem. At the same time, however, by distinguishing three rather than two levels, it goes beyond the framework of Cartesian dualism and opens up an entire new set of problems, concerning the relation between what is properly human and what is properly divine. Swedenborg's solution of the Cartesian dilemma—by suggesting that there is a relation of correspondence rather than of causal influence[22] between soul and body—remains important for understanding the genesis of his worldview, and a broadly Cartesian framework remains visible, for example, in Swedenborg's insistence that "nature is dead."[23] But *Secrets of Heaven* is no longer much concerned with investigating that physical world. The attention now shifts to the human and divine levels, and Swedenborg's mature worldview is carried by the conviction that these, too, are not causally related but stand in a relation of correspondence. Having established these intellectual foundations, it is now time to have a closer look at Swedenborg's *magnum opus*.

2

The Structure of *Secrets of Heaven*

Swedenborg's *Secrets of Heaven* was written during the period 1748–1756, and was published anonymously in eight volumes over eight years from 1749 on. The complete work consists of 10,837 numbered sections of varying length, plus four short, unnumbered prefaces.

In order to find one's way through this massive work, it is necessary first of all to see that it consists of three interwoven but autonomous strands. The shortest one consists of "introductory parts" about matters of method, history, and doctrine, while the longest one consists of a systematic and extremely detailed exegesis of Genesis and Exodus (including complete translations of both)[24] and a strand of intermediate but substantial length referred to as *Memorabilia*, or memorable occurrences: accounts of Swedenborg's experiences in the spiritual world. The contents of the three strands can be analyzed as follows:[25]

The First Strand: Method, History, and Doctrine

[Unnumbered introductory note]. The essential nature of the Word: §§1–5. The inner life of the Word: §§64–66. Secrets of the other life: §§67–72. Representations of inner meaning: §§166–167. Author's preface [to volume 2]. The Word's inner meaning: §§1886–1889, 1984. Author's preface [to Genesis 18]. More on the Word's inner meaning: §§2135, 2310–2311, 2495, 2606–2609. Author's preface [to volume 3]. The white horse: §§2760–2763. History of the Word: §§2894–2900. The name Jesus Christ: §§3004–3011. Narrative detail in the Word: §§3228–3229. Matthew 24: §§3353–3356, 3486–3489,

3650–3655, 3751–3757, 3897–3901, 4056–4060, 4229–4231, 4332–4335, 4422–4424. The close of the age: §4535. Matthew 25: §§4635–4638, 4661–4664, 4807–4810, 4954–4959, 5063–5071. Teachings on charity: §§6627–6633

Teachings about Charity: §§6703–6712, 6818–6824, 6933–6938, 7080–7086, 7178–7182, 7255–7263, 7366–7377, 7488–7494, 7623–7627, 7752–7762, 7814–7821, 8033–8037, 8120–8124, 8252–8257, 8387–8394, 8548–8553, 8635–8640, 8742–8747, 8853–8858, 8958–8969, 9112–9122

Teachings about Charity and Faith: §§9239–9245, 9363–9369, 9443–9454, 9585–9591, 9701–9709, 9796–9803, 9974–9984, 10167–10175, 10318–10325, 10386–10392, 10519–10522, 10591–10597, 10714–10724, 10740–10749, 10760–10766, 10773–10781, 10789–10806, 10815–10831

The Second Strand: Biblical Exegesis

Genesis	Summary	Inner Meaning
1	§§6–13	§§14–63
2:1–17	§§73–80	§§81–130
2:18–25	§§131–136	§§137–167
3:1–13	§§190–193	§§194–233
3:14–19	§§234–240	§§241–279
3:20–24	§§280–285	§§286–313
4	§§324–336	§§337–442
5	§§460–467	§§468–536
6:1–8	§§554–559	§§560–598
6:9–22	§§599–604	§§605–683
7	§§701–704	§§705–813
8	§§832–837	§§838–937
9	§§971–976	§§977–1105
10	§§1130–1138	§§1139–1264
11	§§1279–1282	§§1283–1375
12	§§1401–1402	§§1403–1502[26]

13	§§1535–1539	§§1540–1618
14	§§1651–1658	§§1659–1756
15	§§1778–1782	§§1783–1868
16	§§1890–1891	§§1892–1965
17	§§1985–1986	§§1987–2116
18	§§2136–2141	§§2142–2288
19	§§2312–2316	§§2317–2468
20	§§2496–2497	§§2498–2588
21	§§2610–2614	§§2615–2726
22	§§2764–2765	§§2766–2869
23	§§2901–2902	§§2903–2986
24	§§3012–3014	§§3015–3212
25	§§3230–3233	§§3234–3336
26	§§3357–3361	§§3362–3471
27	§3490	§§3491–3623
28	§§3656–3657	§§3658–3740
29	§§3758–3759	§§3760–3882
30	§§3902–3903	§§3904–4038
31	§4061	§§4062–4217
32	§4232	§§4233–4317
33	§4336	§§4337–4402
34	§4425	§§4426–4522
35	§4536	§§4537–4621
36	§4639	§§4640–4651
37	§4665	§§4666–4790
38	§§4811–4812	§§4813–4930
39	§§4960–4961	§§4962–5049
40	§5072	§§5073–5170
41	§§5191–5192	§§5193–5376
42	§§5396b[27]–5397	§§5398–5551
43	§5574	§§5575–5710
44	§§5728–5730	§§5731–5845
45	§5867	§§5868–5975
46	§5994	§§5995–6052
47	§§6059–6061	§§6062–6188
48	§§6216–6217	§§6218–6306

| 49 | §§6328–6332 | §§6333–6465 |
| 50 | §6497 | §§6498–6597 |

Exodus	Summary	Inner Meaning
1	§§6634–6635	§§6636–6694
2	§§6713–6714	§§6715–6806
3	§6825	§§6826–6920
4	§§6939–6941	§§6942–7068
5	§7087	§§7088–7169
6	§§7183–7184	§§7185–7245b[28]
7	§§7264–7265	§§7266–7357
8	§7378	§§7379–7474
9	§7495	§§7496–7619
10	§7628	§§7629–7741
11	§7763	§§7764–7798
12	§§7822–7823	§§7824–8020
13	§§8038–8039	§§8040–8110
14	§8125	§§8126–8241
15	§§8258–8259	§§8260–8370
16	§8395	§§8396–8540
17	§§8554–8555	§§8556–8626
18	§8641	§§8642–8732
19	§8748	§§8749–8845
20	§8859	§§8860–8946
21	§8970	§§8971–9103
22	§9123	§§9124–9231
23	§9246	§§9247–9349
24	§9370	§§9371–9437
25	§9455	§§9456–9577
26	§9592	§§9593–9692
27	§§9710–9712	§§9713–9789
28	§9804	§§9805–9966
29	§9985	§§9986–10158
30	§10175a[29]	§§10176–10310
31	§10326	§§10327–10376
32	§§10393–10394	§§10395–10512

33	§10523	§§10524–10584
34	§§10589–10600	§§10601–10707
35	§10725	§§10726–10733
36	§10750	—
37	§10767	—
38	§10782	—
39	§10807	—
40	§10832	—

The Third Strand: Accounts of Memorable Occurrences

Death. Our resurrection from death and entry into eternal life: §§68–189, 314–319. What the life of the soul or spirit is then like: §§320–323. Several examples from spirits of opinions they adopted during their physical lives concerning the soul or spirit: §§443–448

Heaven. Heaven and heavenly joy: §§449–459, 537–553. The communities that make up heaven: §§684–691

Hell. §§692–700. The hells of those who spent their lives in hatred, revenge, and cruelty: §§814–823. The hells of those who spent their lives in adultery and lechery; the hells of deceivers and witches: §§824–831. Misers' hells; the foul Jerusalem and robbers in the wilderness; the feces-laden hells of those who have pursued sensual pleasure alone: §§938–946. Other hells: §§947–970

Spiritual devastation. §§1106–1113

Antedeluvian history. The earliest church: §§1114–1129. The pre-Flood people who died out: §§1265–1272

The world of spirits and angels. Location in the "universal human"; place, distance, and time in the other life: §§1273–1278, 1376–1382. The ability of spirits and angels to perceive things;

auras in the other life: §§1383–1400, 1504–1520. The light angels live in; their magnificent gardens and their dwellings: §§1521–1534, 1619–1633. The way spirits and angels talk: §§1634–1650, 1757–1764. Sacred Scripture, or the Word, which conceals a divine message that lies open to the view of good spirits and angels: §§1767–1777, 1869–1885

Visions, dreams, prophecy. §§1966–1983

The Last Judgment. §§2117–2134

The state of children in the other world. §§2289–2309

The power of recall that we keep after death. §§2469–2494

The lot and condition in the other world of nations and peoples born outside the church. §§2589–2605

The way marriage and adultery are viewed in heaven. §§2727–2759

Human freedom. §§2870–2893

Representation and correspondence. §§2987–3003, 3213–3227, 3337–3352, 3472–3485

The universal human. §§3624–3649, 3741–3750, 3883–3896, 4039–4055, 4218–4228, 4318–4331, 4403–4421, 4523–4534, 4622–4634, 4652–4660, 4791–4806, 4931–4953, 5050–5062, 5171–5190, 5377–5396, 5552–5573

Disease. §§5711–5727

The angels and spirits with us. §§5846–5866, 5976–5993

Spiritual influence, and soul-body interaction. §§6053–6058, 6189–6215, 6307–6327, 6466–6496, 6598–6626

The inhabitants of other planets. §§6695–6702. Mercury: §§6807–6817, 6921–6932, 7069–7079, 7170–7177. Venus: §§7246–7254. Mars: §§7358–7365, 7475–7487, 7620–7622, 7742–7751. Jupiter: §§7799–7813, 8021–8032, 8111–8119, 8242–8251, 8371–8386, 8541–8547, 8627–8634, 8733–8741, 8846–8852. Saturn: §§8947–8957, 9104–9111. The moon: §§9232–9238. Why the Lord wanted to be born on our planet and not another: §§9350–9362. Planets in outer space; their inhabitants, spirits, and angels: §§9438–9442. First planet: §§9578–9584, 9693–9700, 9790–9795. Second planet: §§9967–9973, 10159–10166. Third planet: §§10311–10317, 10377-10385, 10513-10518. Fourth planet: §§10585–10590, 10708–10713. Fifth planet: §§10734–10739, 10751–10759, 10768–10772. Sixth planet: §§10783–10788, 10808–10814a, 10833–10837

The first strand, that of the "introductory parts," is divided into two sections. It is logical that Swedenborg sets this strand apart from the two others, for here he discusses and seeks to legitimize the basic assumptions on which the entire work is founded. The first part of this strand is theoretical and methodological, containing explanations and justifications of his general approach to biblical exegesis. This part can be further analyzed, as will be seen, into discussions of method and discussions of history. The second part is doctrinal and focuses on the theological concepts of charity and faith.

The second and the third of the three strands focus on the two levels of reality that, as explained in the previous chapter, are basic to *Secrets of Heaven*:

Divine	Strand 3: Accounts of Memorable Occurrences
Human	Strand 2: Biblical Exegesis
Physical	—

The second strand, that of biblical exegesis, is quantitatively the longest. It consists of an extremely detailed interpretation of how the Lord manifests himself on the intermediate, human level, that is to say, through the

Bible. Referring to my musical analogy, Genesis and Exodus can be compared to two great symphonies, the divine meaning of which is decoded by Swedenborg note by note and melody by melody; the role he assumes might be compared to that of a divinely inspired musicologist, who analyzes the symphonies not just according to worldly canons but discloses their "real meaning" as revealed to him from up above.

The third strand, the memorable occurrences, is shorter but still of very substantial length and is based upon Swedenborg's direct experiences of the higher, heavenly, or "inner" level of reality. Here we are not dealing with interpretations but with direct accounts of "things heard and seen." The physical level to which Swedenborg had devoted most of his early career is not systematically treated in *Secrets of Heaven*, although some discussions pertaining to physics can be found scattered through the work. We will now proceed to a separate discussion of each of the three strands.

3

Method, History, and Doctrine

IN THIS CHAPTER, WE WILL FIRST BE LOOKING AT HOW SWEDENBORG describes the method of exegesis that he uses in the second strand of *Secrets of Heaven*. Next, we will discuss his beliefs about the historical development of religious consciousness. Finally, we will analyze his doctrine of "Charity and Faith."

The Method of Biblical Exegesis

The first sentence of *Secrets of Heaven* contains in a nutshell the thesis fundamental to the whole work:

> The Word in the Old Testament contains the mysteries of heaven, and every single aspect of it has to do with the Lord, his heaven, the church, faith, and all the tenets of faith; but not a single person sees this in the letter. (§1)

Here we are introduced right away to Swedenborg's basic assumption about biblical exegesis: Scripture, or the Word, has an "inner meaning" that cannot be grasped from the outer, or literal, meaning,[30] and therefore a correct interpretation of the Bible requires divine revelation. Only "very few" people have been granted such revelation, and Swedenborg is one of them:

> The Lord in his divine mercy has granted me the opportunity for several years now, without break or interruption, to mingle among spirits and angels, to hear them talking, and to speak with them in turn. Consequently I have been able to see and hear the

most amazing things in the other life, which have never before
come into people's awareness or into their power to visualize.
(*Secrets of Heaven* §5)

Swedenborg is not content with merely making a categorical statement
about his unique status and authority as interpreter of the Bible. While
the inner meaning of Scripture cannot be inferred from the literal meaning and therefore has to be revealed, the fact that an inner meaning exists
can be rationally deduced by anybody who believes that the Bible is God's
Word. For how else could one explain that it contains so many passages
that are simply unintelligible if taken literally, and others that describe
things so "abominable" as to be clearly far below God's dignity? This point
is repeated many times, and must be seen as a major impetus behind his
gigantic exegetic labors: to Swedenborg's critical, rational, and scientifically
trained mind, conventional ideas of the Bible as God's Word just did not
make any sense. What, for example, can one make of an evidently nonsensical sentence found in Genesis 49:17: "Dan shall be a snake by the road-
side, a viper along the path, that bites the horse's heels so that its rider falls
backward"?[31] And what about passages that may be intelligible in themselves, but are mediocre, useless, or even offensive?

Would anyone expect God's Word to mention the disgusting
affair of Lot's daughters? . . . How about the story in which Jacob
peeled the bark off some rods, laying them bare down to the white
and placing them in the water troughs to make the flock bear
mottled, speckled, and spotted lambs? . . . They would lack any
importance; it would be all the same whether we knew them or
not, if they did not enfold a divine secret deep inside them. Otherwise they would not differ in any way from other histories.[32]
(*Secrets of Heaven* §2310:3)

The new rationalist Bible criticism that emerged during Swedenborg's lifetime would, of course, come to that precise conclusion. Swedenborg, however, reasoned differently. If one assumes that the Bible is divinely inspired
from the first word to the last and acknowledges at the same time that this
is not borne out by the text's literal meaning, the only solution is to assume
that it simply does not mean what it seems to mean. The Bible *has* to

contain "secrets" (*arcana*) that contain its actual hidden life; without that life, it cannot be the Word of the Lord (*Secrets of Heaven* §2). In choosing this formulation, Swedenborg explicitly draws an analogy with biological organisms. A mere material body is dead; it can be called a living being only if it has a soul in it (§3). Likewise, the outer letter of the Bible is dead; it can only be the Word of the Lord—who is Life himself—if it contains a hidden dimension of life.

This hidden dimension cannot be inferred from the literal text at all. As will be seen, Swedenborg treats Genesis and Exodus as gigantic coded texts, the actual meaning of which must be disclosed by a process of decoding. Every single word means something else than what it means on the surface. Technically this procedure is a clear example, albeit in an extreme form, of what is known as allegorical exegesis.[33] Traditional biblical hermeneutics distinguished generally between the *sensus literalis* or *historicus* (literal or historical sense) of the Bible, on the one hand, and the *sensus spiritualis* or *mysticus* (spiritual or mystical sense) that largely relied on various types of allegorical exegesis, on the other.[34] Allegorical exegesis came to be applied to the Old Testament as early as several centuries B.C.E.; it was promoted as the central method of biblical exegesis by the Jewish philosopher Philo of Alexandria (ca. 20 BCE–50 CE) in the first century CE and by the Christian theologian Origen (185–ca. 254) in the third, and became the standard approach throughout the Middle Ages (Longenecker 1975, 45–48). This dominance came under sharp attack during the Reformation: the doctrine of *sola scriptura* implied that only the *sensus literalis/historicus* was to be accepted. Martin Luther (1483–1546) sharply attacked Origen's approach, and John Calvin (1509–1564) did the same in an even more uncompromising manner. As explained by Hans-Joachim Kraus in his standard history of the historical-critical study of the Old Testament, according to the Lutherans and Calvinists,

> with any allegorical interpretation, the human voice imperceptibly mixes itself through God's speech. Within the wide space of allegorical possibilities of interpretation, Man with his ideas settles down and claims his rights—in a place where he should keep silent, and merely listen and ask. Whoever seeks for allegories in the Bible, leaves the solid ground of the letter and of history. . . . In allegory, the Word of God is turned into a fictitious word of

Man. Therefore the warning call is "Cavete ab allegoriis!" (Beware of allegories). For example when 1 Corinthians 10:4 says "and that rock was Christ," Luther explicitly points out that here, too, there should be no room for "allegoria or spiritual interpretation." He continues: "It was not a case of figurative speech, but a matter of great seriousness, God's word, that gives life, and the right faith was there. Therefore this did not just seem to happen to them [the apostles], but it really happened." From this passage . . . one can see how Luther smells in any allegory the acute danger that the historical reality of God's Word will be dissolved into general meaning-contents, and thus into unsubstantial illusions. (Kraus 1982, 14)

One might perceive an irony in the fact that Swedenborg, whose religious worldview was developed entirely from Lutheran foundations (although, of course, he eventually went far beyond them) and for whom Roman Catholicism was self-evidently a perversion of the original Christian message, came to reject these fundamental Lutheran principles in favor of an exegetical method that returns straight to Philo, Origen, and mainstream medieval biblical hermeneutics.[35] Philo, for example,

was prepared to interpret allegorically anything that might derogate the dignity of the inspired words of God: anything that is nonsensical in the creation accounts, that is reprehensible in the legal portions, or that is trivial in the historical narratives of the Pentateuch. . . . The *prima facie* meaning must normally be pushed aside—even counted as offensive—to make room for the intended spiritual meaning underlying the obvious; though . . . at times he seems willing to consider literal and allegorical exegesis as having "parallel legitimacy." In the main, however, exegesis of Holy Writ was for him an esoteric enterprise which, while not without its governing principles, was to be dissociated from literal interpretation. (Longenecker 1975, 46)

Except for minor details, these lines could as well have been written about Swedenborg. In his standard biography, Martin Lamm concluded not only that Swedenborg's exegetical method is "exactly the one Philo of Alexandria and Origen followed," but also that the concrete exegetical results are often identical: a comparison between Philo's and Swedenborg's interpretations of certain specific passages in Genesis showed striking affinities (Lamm [1915] 2000, 227–231). Having pointed out that this does not need to imply Swedenborg's direct dependence on Philo, Lamm concluded that Swedenborg must be seen as the "late inheritor" of an uninterrupted exegetical tradition:

> The only difference between [Swedenborg's] results and those of his predecessors is, all in all, that his results have been adapted to his philosophical system, whereas the latter have allowed their explications to illustrate their respective systems. Like his forerunners, Swedenborg so freely used allegorical interpretation to reshape the meaning of Scripture that it became possible for him to incorporate his whole philosophical system in his exegesis and to form a logically consistent theological doctrine out of this hermeneutical operation. When he repeatedly stresses in his theological works that he has learned all the teachings of his church from reading the Word, he is certainly sincere. All the same, it is quite the opposite. He has independently formed a philosophical-theological view that he then point for point finds corroborated in his biblical studies. (Lamm [1915] 2000, 231–232)

Lamm slightly overstates his case here and creates some confusion by assuming a contradiction that is actually only apparent. Claiming that anything one knows comes only from reading the Bible is a commonplace of Protestant pious discourse; but Swedenborg never meant to imply that he had learned his teachings by reading the Word unaided. On the contrary, he claims that its true meaning was revealed to him by the Lord; in other words, it was only thanks to direct divine inspiration that he was able, as formulated by Lamm in the above quotation, to "learn all the teachings of his church from reading the Word." It is true that Swedenborg's approach can technically be categorized as "allegorical," but it differs from the allegorical tradition more strongly than Lamm suggests. The key to Swedenborg's specificity is, precisely, his Protestantism. While Roman Catholicism had always assigned to the *pietas fidelium* ("the piety of the faithful," that is to say, the tradition of pious consensus) an authority equal to that of the Bible, Swedenborg's attitude is strongly marked by the characteristic Protestant emphasis on the Bible as the sole and exclusive source of divine revelation. Not unlike Luther himself, Swedenborg had emerged from his religious crisis with a profound feeling of the absolute sovereignty of the Lord and his Word: instead of listening to our own merely human opinions, clinging to our own pet ideas (scientific and rationalist ones in his case) and thereby "mixing our own voice through God's speech,"[36] we must wholly submit to the Lord and allow him to guide us in every respect. This quintessentially Protestant ethos permeates Swedenborg's dream diary (see Swedenborg 2001) and is essential for understanding his *Secrets of Heaven*. From such a perspective, the task of trying to understand the Lord's Word must receive a new urgency and lead to an approach that is qualitatively different from the somewhat more relaxed attitude of the traditional allegorists in the Roman Catholic tradition. In reading the Bible, they could allow themselves to be guided by the *pietas fidelium*, in which the Holy Spirit was believed to be invisibly at work. But for Swedenborg, as for Luther, traditional opinion was the product of mere human thinking and had no divine authority whatsoever; the individual creature finds himself face to face with the Lord Himself, who communicates with him through his Word. This Word is clear and unequivocal. It does not have many layers of meaning, as in traditional allegorical exegesis, but only two: the outer and the inner.[37] The inner meaning is no longer understood by human beings, and therefore the Lord himself now reveals it again to humankind through his chosen instrument Emanuel Swedenborg.

Paradoxically, then, Swedenborg's allegorical exegesis of the Bible is a radical but entirely logical outcome of Protestant biblicism. It reflects a profoundly felt wish to listen to the Lord's pure and unadulterated Word. Human opinions and traditions are suspect in principle and are not allowed to interfere. The great Bible Code can be broken only by the Lord himself.

History and the Styles of the Word

That a historical-critical approach to the Bible always remained alien to Swedenborg is evident, for example, from this passage about how he perceived the thoughts of biblical scholars after death:

Some people during bodily life had devoted themselves exclusively to biblical criticism when reading the Word, without much concern for the meaning, and their thoughts were represented as lines that were shut off rather than open-ended, and woven into a network.

Some of these people were once with me, and everything I thought and wrote became tangled in confusion. My thinking was virtually imprisoned, because they narrowed it down to the words themselves, turning my attention away from the meaning so forcefully that they completely wore me out. Yet they considered themselves wiser than others![38] (*Secrets of Heaven* §6621)

Swedenborg did, however, attempt to differentiate among various "styles" in the Bible, and connect them with different historical stages in the development of human and religious consciousness. Most sublime is the style of the "earliest church," about which more will be said below. The first chapters of the Bible—the stories concerning the creation, the Garden of Eden, and everything else up to the time of Abraham—are written in this style. On the face of it, they may seem to be about earthly and worldly things, but in fact everything in them should be understood only in a spiritual and heavenly manner: by means of a narrative or quasi-historical sequence, the members of the earliest church presented inner truths, and this gave them "the fullest pleasure possible" (*Secrets of Heaven* §66:1). Because the parts of the Bible written in this style should not be taken literally at all, they are different from those written in the "narrative" or "historical" style. The stories from Abraham onwards and the books of Joshua, Judges, Samuel, and Kings are historically accurate *and* have an inner meaning: "The historical events in these books are exactly what they appear to be in the literal sense, but as a whole and in detail they still contain an entirely different meaning on the inner plane" (*Secrets of Heaven* §66:2). A third, "prophetical," style is described by Swedenborg as an offspring of the style of the earliest church, but as differing from it because it is not continuous and does not take a quasi-historical form. Parts written in this style only make sense from the internal perspective, for if taken literally they are "choppy, and almost completely unintelligible." Finally, there is the style of the Psalms of David, which "is midway between the prophetic style and people's usual way of speaking" (§66:2).

These statements should be seen in connection with *Secrets of Heaven*
§10325, where Swedenborg says explicitly that only those books that have
the inner meaning belong to the Word and lists all of them. According to
Swedenborg, the Old Testament Word consists of only the five Books of
Moses, Joshua, Judges, 1 and 2 Samuel, 1 and 2 Kings, the Psalms, Isaiah,
Jeremiah, Lamentations, Ezekiel, Daniel, Hosea, Joel, Amos, Obadiah,
Jonah, Micah, Nahum, Habakkuk, Zephaniah, Haggai, Zechariah, and
Malachi. Within the New Testament, he accepts only the four Gospels and
the Book of Revelation. This means, of course, that such traditionally
important parts of the Bible as, for example, the Old Testament book of
Job or the Song of Solomon, and most of the New Testament (including
the Acts of the Apostles and all the Epistles) were considered by Swedenborg as not directly inspired by heaven. This fact has worried some of Swedenborg's admirers. For example, on March 18, 1766, Gabriel Beyer asked
Swedenborg for clarification about the letters of the apostles and Paul; Swedenborg responded on April 15:

> In respect to the writings of the apostles and Paul, I have not
> quoted them in the *Arcana Coelestia*, because they are doctrinal
> writings, and consequently are not written in the style of the
> Word, like those of the prophets, of David, of the Evangelists,
> and the Book of Revelation. The style of the Word consists alto-
> gether of correspondences, wherefore it is effective of immedi-
> ate communication with heaven; but in doctrinal writings there
> is a different style, which has indeed communication with heaven,
> but mediately. . . . The writings of the apostles are, nevertheless,
> good books of the church, insisting upon the doctrine of charity
> and its faith as strongly as the Lord Himself has done in the
> Gospels and the Book of Revelation; as may be seen and found
> evident by every one who in reading them directs his attention
> to these points.[39]

Apart from the four biblical "styles," Swedenborg also distinguishes between
a sequence of four historical "churches" (that is, prior to the fifth, new
church) each one of which had its own "Word":

> To speak more specifically, the Word has existed at every period, though not the Word we have today. The earliest church, which came before the Flood, had one form. The ancient church, which followed the Flood, had another. The Jewish religion had the Word written by Moses and the prophets. And lastly the new church had the Word written by the Gospel writers. (*Secrets of Heaven* §2895)

The members of the earliest church, before the Flood, were "heavenly people" who lived in daily company with the angels. They had no priests or external cult, nor did they need a written Word: their "Adamic intellect"[40] allowed them to communicate directly with the angels and have an intuitive grasp of the divine truth. Thus, they knew by direct perception what was good and true and had the Word "written on their hearts." They perceived worldly things by the senses and simultaneously understood them spiritually: "everything they saw (or sensed in any other way) represented and symbolized the heavenly and spiritual qualities of the Lord's kingdom to them" (§2896).

The members of the "ancient church," after the Flood, were spiritual but no longer heavenly,[41] and as a result they "learned rather than perceived what the representations and symbolisms involved" (§2897:1). The perfect love and knowledge that had characterized the members of the earliest church had begun to degenerate; and since they could no longer grasp the truth intuitively, the members of this second church had to rely on faith. In order to read the signs of God in nature, they developed an elaborate system of signs, images, emblems, and hieroglyphs. The ancient church fell into decay when the leaders began to misuse their knowledge of the hieroglyphs to promote their own power, as a result of which their priestly office declined to magical superstition, idolatrous cults, and polytheism. Thus, the sacred science of hieroglyphs, which had originally been based on the true correspondence of heaven and earth, was perverted into a tool for demonic sorcery. They did have a written Word, containing historical and prophetical parts, but this Word has gotten lost. Its historical parts were called *Jehovah's Wars*; they were "written in a prophetical style and were for the most part fictional" (§2897:1) like those of Genesis 1–11 in our present Bible.[42] The prophetical parts were called *Utterances* and were

(like the historical parts) written in a style similar to the prophetical style
in our Old Testament. Swedenborg derives the titles of these two parts of
the ancient Word (*Liber Bellorum Jehovae* and *Enuntiata*) from Numbers
21:14 and 27.

With the revelation of the Ten Commandments followed the third, or
"Jewish church" (§2899), which represents a further stage of decline. The
Jewish law and sacrificial cult are merely outward representations, but at
least they contain the authentic divine truth; as Ernst Benz has put it in
his important Swedenborg biography, they are "a trick of reason" by which
the inner divine truths were preserved for posterity in outward forms and
symbols, even though the members of the Jewish church themselves were
no longer capable of understanding what these symbols meant. Thus, the
Jewish church was "a last resort in the era of the general decline of religion"
(Benz [1969] 2002, 456). Their Word was, of course, the Old Testament;
and the meaning of its "representations and symbols" is the subject of Swedenborg's *Secrets of Heaven*. The Jewish church came to its end with the
destruction of Jerusalem and the diaspora (*Secrets of Heaven* §4057).

The Christian church is the fourth one in line. Christ did away with the
worship of mere outward show and refocused attention on the inward truths
of faith. However, this did not lead to the return of the Golden Age, for
the human race was no longer able to understand the truth as it was revealed
to them. In fact, only the original apostolic congregation was still pure; and
with the development of Roman Catholicism, the Christian church quickly
degenerated into what would eventually be a travesty of the true church.
The Protestant Reformation, with its emphasis on literal interpretation,
has not succeeded in leading the church back to the true understanding of
the Word. The Word of the fourth church obviously consists of the New
Testament added to the Old Testament. Christ spoke "from divinity itself.
Everything he said, then, also represented and symbolized divine concerns
and therefore the heavenly concerns of his kingdom and church" (§2900).

Swedenborg's revelations now mark the beginning of the fifth, or "new,"
church, which will be established among the few who "can now be taught,"
but whom only the Lord knows. Of these "chosen," who lead a good life
based on faith and love, few will be found in the present church; for in the
past, too, it has always been among people outside the church that new
religions were established.[43]

Having distinguished four "styles" of the Word, as well as four churches prior to the appearance of the new church, Swedenborg furthermore describes how each church goes through four "stages of corruption":[44]

> first of all, people started to forget what was good and true and quarreled over it; second, they developed contempt for it; third, they refused to acknowledge it; fourth, they profaned it. (*Secrets of Heaven* §3899)

After the fourth and final state of perversion of a church, a new one is instituted. From *Secrets of Heaven*, it is evident that Swedenborg saw his own writings as heralding the new church. Only towards the end of his life, however, would he make the radical claim that they were in fact the new Word and that their publication represented what was meant by the Second Coming.[45]

Teachings about Charity and Faith

Having discussed the stages of perversion of a church by means of a detailed exegesis of Matthew 24, Swedenborg moves on to Matthew 25 in order to discuss the meaning of the Second Coming and the fate of the soul after death. The Coming of the Son of Man should not be taken literally: it refers not to a judgment at the end of history, but to what happens to every individual person after death. Swedenborg takes the occasion to polemicize against the Protestant doctrine of salvation by faith alone: "The fruit of faith is simply a life in keeping with the commandments of faith, so it is clearly such a life that saves us, not our beliefs apart from the way we live" (*Secrets of Heaven* §4663). This leads him to a preliminary discussion of the "essential ingredients of charity" as listed in Matthew 25:35–36: "[F]or I was hungry and you gave me food, I was thirsty and you gave me something to drink, I was a stranger and you welcomed me, I was naked and you gave me clothing, I was sick and you took care of me, I was in prison and you visited me" (§4954).

This turns out to be the upbeat for the extensive discussions of "charity and faith" that take up the remainder of what we have referred to as the "first strand" of *Secrets of Heaven*. Implicit in these discussions is a general

framework of correspondences and associations that may be presented in
a systematic form, and that guides discussions throughout *Secrets of
Heaven*:[46]

Heavenly	The Lord	Love (Warmth)	Good	Will
Spiritual	Neighbor			
		Faith (Light)	Truth	Intellect

What we have here is the basic Swedenborgian concept of love and faith
as ultimately inseparable, but analytically distinguishable as the "higher"
and the "lower" dimension, respectively, of one and the same divine reality:

> The material world has two components to its life force: warmth
> and light. The spiritual world has two components to it: love
> and faith. Warmth in the material world corresponds to love in
> the spiritual world, and light in the material world corresponds
> to faith existing in the spiritual world. That is why love is meant
> when spiritual warmth or fire is mentioned, and faith is meant
> when spiritual light is mentioned. . . . The world's sun generates
> the warmth and light of the material world, but heaven's sun gen-
> erates spiritual warmth and light, or love and faith. Heaven's sun
> is the Lord. The warmth radiating from him as the sun is love,
> and the light radiating from him as the sun is faith. (*Secrets of
> Heaven* §§7082–7083)

If we follow Swedenborg in his biblical exegesis as well as in his memorable occurrences, we see how all other dimensions of the spiritual world
and of morality are structured around this basic distinction. Swedenborg

begins by pointing out that, among the people of the ancient church, there were differences of opinion regarding matters of faith, but that these were considered of secondary importance: "People acknowledged all who led a good, charitable life as members of the church and called them sister or brother, no matter how strongly they disagreed on the truth that is now called religious truth" (§6628). In other words, charity took precedence over faith.

The commandment to "love one's neighbor" is discussed in detail. The people of the ancient church distinguished various categories of "neighbor" and had precise guidelines about how charity should be exercised towards each of these categories.[47] The Lord himself is the neighbor in the highest degree; everybody else is the neighbor in the measure that the Lord resides in him; and everybody is also his own neighbor. This last dimension of the command, however, ranks lowest: of course, one must provide oneself with the necessities of life in order to be in a condition to exercise charity towards others, but the basic commandment—repeated many times by Swedenborg—is that "self-love and love for the world," which are the roots of all evil, must be overcome in favor of "love for one's neighbor and for the Lord." These two loves are of a different kind: the first and lower one, love for one's neighbor, is called "spiritual" while the second and higher one, love for the Lord, is called "heavenly." This same basic distinction between spiritual and heavenly recurs in Swedenborg's description of the structure of heaven, as will be seen.

Crucial to Swedenborg's moral teaching is his doctrine of dominant or ruling loves. Neither our beliefs nor our outward behavior is essential to our salvation (that is to say, the Protestant doctrine of justification by faith alone is rejected along with the Roman Catholic emphasis on good works); what matters is the inner motivational drive, or ruling love, that guides our actions and behavior. We are each ultimately motivated by "love for that which we hold as our goal" (§7081), and only this ruling or dominant love molds our character and determines our fate after death. For example, it does not matter if we have done many good deeds during our life, if we did them out of self-love or love for the world (for example, because we wanted to be praised as benefactors of humanity). We must do it out of genuine love for our neighbor and for the Lord. Even worse is the Protestant idea of justification by faith, regardless of love:

Faith devoid of love resembles light devoid of warmth, which is
what winter light is like. Faith combined with love resembles light
combined with warmth, which is what the light of spring is like.
It is known that everything grows and flourishes in spring's light,
and that everything droops and dies in winter's light. The same
holds true for faith and love. (*Secrets of Heaven* §7084)

There are two mental powers in a person: intellect and will. The will has
been given to humans for the sake of the good of love, the intellect for the
sake of the truth of faith. It is not possible to separate the two, that is to
say, to "understand and speak truth while willing and doing evil (§7180)."
If a person were to do this, one mental power would be looking upward
towards heaven and another downward towards hell, and the person would
be suspended between them. Such a thing cannot and does not happen,
simply because the will (linked to love and the good) has precedence over
the intellect (linked to faith and truth): "The will carries a person along,
with the intellect in support" (§7180).[48]

   Swedenborg's discussions become slightly more complicated because he
sometimes speaks of "love" (*amor*), sometimes of "charity" (*charitas*), while
using both terms in combination with only one theoretical counterpart:
"faith" (*fides*). Charity and faith, and the relation between them, are
described with characteristic scholastic precision:

Charity is an inner passion consisting in a heartfelt desire to do
good to one's neighbor as the greatest pleasure in one's life and
to do so without reward. . . . Faith, on the other hand, is an inner
passion consisting in a heartfelt desire to know what is true and
good, not for the sake of doctrine as the ultimate goal but for the
sake of life. What ties this passion to that of charity is the desire
to behave according to the truth and therefore to actually do the
truth. (*Secrets of Heaven* §§8033–8034)

One might wonder how this definition of charity, as an "inner passion"
and a "desire" that springs from the heart, can be combined with Swedenborg's insistence on the will. Exerting one's will so as to act charitably is
not sufficient for salvation because it concerns only the external. Is it really

possible, however, to change one's heart and one's inward passions or desires by a sheer act of will? Answering that question brings us to Swedenborg's doctrine of regeneration.

Swedenborg states that, in order to enter heaven, one must be "born anew from the Lord" by "accept[ing] spiritual life" (§8548). However, nobody is born with such spiritual life, for from one's parents one receives only physical life. We are all born in what would traditionally be called a "state of sin":

> We are each born into the evils of self-love and materialism passed on by our parents. Every fault that we take on as second nature through habit we pass on to our offspring, as part of a long sequence reaching back to our parents, grandparents, and great-grandparents. Our resulting inheritance of evil eventually grows so large that our own, independent spark of life is nothing but evil through and through. This unending chain is not broken or altered except by a life of faith and neighborly love received from the Lord. (*Secrets of Heaven* §8550)

Like John Locke (1632–1704), one of the major influences on his thought, Swedenborg adamantly rejected the philosophical doctrine of "innate ideas,"[49] believing instead that, at birth, a person is a *tabula rasa*, and gaining knowledge is dependent on the senses. Since the senses do not give us access to the inner or heavenly realities, we are dependent in this regard on revelation. As explained by Martin Lamm in his excellent discussion of Swedenborg's doctrine of regeneration, we find ourselves in a state of "permanent equilibrium" between our hereditary tendencies towards evil on the one hand, and God's continuous efforts to show us the way to heaven, on the other (see Lamm 2000, 271–274). When we are in the process of being regenerated, we experience acute temptations, caused by evil spirits who are fighting with good spirits for dominion over our soul. We have to exert our own free will to allow the "new birth" to take place within us by choosing the side of heaven, in a constant battle with our evil tendencies and the temptation by evil spirits. It is initially by means of faith, aided by reason, that we accept the new truth shown to us; and as part of this process, "charity is planted [deeper and deeper] . . . until it takes over" (§8856).

Once this happens, charity has become our "true will," and this remains unchangeable after death (§8853–8858, 8958–8969). Swedenborg was convinced that he had undergone this very process of regeneration during the time of his spiritual crisis; it was only thanks to the Lord having fought for him that he was able finally to gain the victory.[50] In sum, human beings cannot be reborn without help from the Lord, but it is up to us to make the decisive step of choosing the good.

The remaining parts of the "first strand" of *Secrets of Heaven* are devoted to a series of specific subjects, some of which have already been touched upon before and some of which would be developed at much greater length in Swedenborg's later works. These subjects include the meaning of the forgiveness of sins, freedom and free will, marriage love, baptism, the Holy Supper, the body and outer appearance of spirits after death, providence, secular authorities (laws, rewards and punishments, priests, officers, monarchs, and so on), and finally the nature of God, the correct understanding of the Trinity, and the Lord's passion and glorification. If read against the theoretical background outlined above, these parts speak for themselves and therefore need not be summarized here.

4

Biblical Exegesis

To understand the motivation behind Swedenborg's gigantic exegetical labors on Genesis and Exodus, we must keep in mind that the Word was for him quite literally "the means for uniting heaven and earth." It "comes from the Lord and was sent down to us through heaven" and was "written not only for people on earth but also for the angels present with us, . . . which is why the Word has the nature it does and why it is unlike any other piece of literature" (*Secrets of Heaven* §2310).

There is, in fact, a dramatic difference between how angels perceive the Word and how human beings perceive it. Angels perceive the inner meaning and nothing else:

> They know nothing whatever of the literal contents, or the most obvious meaning of even one word, still less the names of different lands, cities, rivers, and people that come up so frequently in the narrative and prophetic parts. All they picture are the things those words and names symbolize. Adam in Paradise, for instance, brings the earliest church to their minds—and not even the church but its belief in the Lord. Noah brings up the picture of that church's remnant among its successors, lasting up to Abram's time. Abram never makes them think of the man who lived but of a saving faith, which he represented. And so on. . . .
>
> Several people found themselves carried up into heaven's outermost entry hall while I was reading the Word, and they spoke to me from there. They said that they had no inkling of a single word or letter there but saw only the things symbolized on the next deeper level of meaning. These, according to their description,

were so beautiful, followed in such a perfect sequence, and affected them so deeply that they called it glory. (*Secrets of Heaven* §§64–65)[51]

The complete and utter ignorance of the angels concerning the literal meaning finds its exact counterpart in the no less radical ignorance of human beings concerning the inner meaning. As pointed out earlier, and as repeated many times by Swedenborg himself, it is indeed impossible to infer the inner meaning from the literal meaning. Each single word functions as a code for an abstract or spiritual concept. To bring this point home, it suffices to give a small sample of some biblical words and their decoded meaning:

Asshur	=	skewed reasoning
Cloud	=	the Word according to its literal meaning
David	=	the Lord
Eagles	=	a person's rational dimension
Ears	=	obedience
Earth	=	the church
Earthquake	=	alteration in the state of the church
Egypt	=	factual information
Eyes	=	intellect
Hand	=	power
Heart	=	desire for good
Heel	=	lowest part of the earthly level
Horse	=	intellect
James	=	charity
John	=	good works
Jewels	=	the tenets of faith
Peter	=	faith
Power and glory	=	the inner meaning
Rider	=	one who has intelligence
Road/path	=	truth
Sea	=	(religious) knowledge
Tyre	=	(religious) knowledge

These examples can be multiplied at will. The undeniable genius of Swedenborg's biblical exegesis—bearing in mind that, from a Swedenborgian perspective, it should be considered as evidence of the divine origin of that exegesis—consists in the fact that his decodings are used consistently throughout *Secrets of Heaven* and that he still manages to come up with a coherent narrative of the inner meaning.

The subject of the Word as a whole, once decoded in this manner, is regeneration (§64); and this process is described as exemplified in the life and inner development of the Lord, on the one hand, and in the historical development of religious consciousness, on the other.[52] As for the book of Genesis, these two strands are distributed as shown in the diagram on the next page. For Exodus the situation is easier: the entire book is devoted to the spiritual church founded by the Lord.

Genesis on the Development of Churches

The account of the six days of creation in Genesis 1 is interpreted as referring to the six consecutive stages in human regeneration: from the initial stage of being "dead" to the stage of a fully developed spiritual person. The seventh day refers to the individual who has progressed from there to the highest stage, that of a "heavenly person," and the description of the Garden of Eden is actually a description of that person's nature and constitution. Swedenborg then reveals that, in fact, this "person" stands for the earliest church and proceeds to describe how this church slowly declined from its original heavenly state. This happened because the members "insisted on autonomy" (*Secrets of Heaven* §137), that is to say, began to let themselves be guided by self-love and love for the world. From this, they began to believe only what their physical senses told them (their sensory part being represented by the serpent in paradise) and to "examine closely the tenets of faith in the Lord, to see whether they were true" (§192). This attitude of criticism and skepticism is represented by eating from the tree of knowledge. They were now under the influence of evil, although an earthly goodness remained with them. No longer willing to believe anything but what they apprehended by the senses, they were well on their way to hell; but to prevent them from having to end up there, the Lord promised that he would come into the world. Swedenborg describes the

Chapter

Spiritual Development of the Lord

Historical Development of Religious Culture

Spiritual Development of the Lord	Chapter	Historical Development of Religious Culture
	1	✓
	2	✓
	3	✓
	4	✓
	5	✓
	6	✓
	7	✓
	8	✓
	9	✓
	10	✓
	11	✓
✓	12	
✓	13	
✓	14	
✓	15	✓
✓	16	
✓	17	
✓	18	
	19	✓
✓	20	
✓	21	
✓	22	
	23	✓
✓	24	
✓	25	✓
✓	26	
✓	27	
✓	28	
✓	29	✓
	30	✓
✓	31	
✓	32	✓
✓	33	
	34	✓
✓	35	
✓	36	
✓	37	
	38	✓
✓	39	
✓	40	
✓	41	
✓	42	
✓	43	
✓	44	✓
✓	45	
✓	46	
✓	47	
	48	✓
	49	✓
	50	✓

Distribution of twin strands concerning regeneration in the chapters of Genesis further degradation of the church, through several generations down to the Flood; the members eventually could no longer apprehend any truth at all, developed an "animalistic nature" (§239), and turned away from everything belonging to faith and love. Cain means "the teaching that faith was separate from love" (§325), while Abel means charity; the murder of the latter by the former means the victory of heretical doctrines over charity. However, a new faith was provided by the Lord, by means of which charity was implanted anew; Seth means this new faith, and Enosh the charity implanted by means of it. Swedenborg continues by describing a number of further churches, represented in the Bible as persons (apart from Seth and Enosh, he mentions Kenan, Mahalalel, Jared, Enoch, Methuselah, Lamech, and Noah). All of these churches derive from the first one called Humankind and are considered branches of the earliest church. From the church called Noah arose three classes of doctrine, referred to as Shem, Ham, and Japheth; they eventually perished in the Flood, that is to say, in a deluge of evil and falsity (§603); but the ark, meaning "a member of this church" (*homo hujus Ecclesiae*, that is, Noah), was saved, thus ensuring the survival of the truth and good residing with him (§639).

Thus ended the earliest church. After the Flood, a new church had to come into existence. This ancient church is referred to as "Noah and his sons." Swedenborg now becomes somewhat less easy to follow in his narrative of this church's development. Its members originally had one doctrine, but they wished "to explore religious truth in a self-directed way" and did so by means of rational argumentation; as a result, they sank into "error and perversions" (§975). In the commentaries to Genesis 10 (§§1131–1137), we find an excellent example of Swedenborg's extreme tendency toward systematic categorization:

- Sons of Japheth: those who engaged in outward worship corresponding to inner worship
- Sons of Gomer and Javan: those who engaged in a form of it that was further removed from inner worship
- "The islands of the nations": those whose worship was even further removed
- Sons of Ham: those who revered knowledge, facts, and ritual and separated them from any deeper properties

- Sons of Cush: those who revered the knowledge of spiritual things
- Sons of Raamah: those who revered the knowledge of heavenly things
- Nimrod: those who engage in outward worship that holds evil and falsity within it
- Descendants of Mizraim: those who take facts, apply logic to them, and in this way invent new forms of worship for themselves; and those who turn religious knowledge into a mere system of fact
- Canaan: outward without inward worship
- Shem: inward worship
- The church established by Eber had outward worship (Joktan) and inward (Peleg)

With Genesis 12, we reach the parts of the Bible written as "true history" (§1401). As we have seen, these parts are to be regarded as historically accurate *and* as carrying an inner meaning. According to the literal meaning, the stories about Abraham, Isaac, and Jacob and what follows describe the third, the "Hebrew church" (§1850:2); but according to the inner meaning, they are about the life of the Lord. We will return to them below.

From this point on, references to the historical "churches" in *Secrets of Heaven* no longer add up to a more or less continuous narrative, but consist of various specific observations about churches. A general line of further development can, however, be distilled from them. After the final decline of the ancient church, a new one was created:

> The new sky and earth were the Hebrew church, which again had its final period, or last judgment, when it became idolatrous. So a new church was raised up, this time among Jacob's descendants. It was called the Jewish religion and was nothing more than a religion that represented charity and faith. In that religion, among Jacob's descendants, there was no charity or faith, so there was also no religion, but only a representation of a religion. The reason was that direct communication of the Lord's kingdom in the heavens with any true religion on earth was impossible, so indirect communication was set up through representations. The final period or last judgment of this so-called

church occurred when the Lord came into the world, because representative acts—specifically sacrifices and other rituals like them—came to an end at that point. The demise of these rituals was achieved by their extermination from the land of Canaan.

Afterward, a new sky and earth were created. That is, a new church was created, which has to be called the nascent [Christian] church. It was started by the Lord and afterward grew gradually stronger, and in its early days it possessed charity and faith. The Lord predicts the death of this church in the Gospels, as does John in the Book of Revelation, and its death is what people call the Last Judgment. Not that heaven and earth will now be obliterated, but that a new church will be raised up in some region of the globe, leaving the current church to remain in its superficial worship, as the Jews remain in theirs. The worship of these people is devoid of charity and faith, or in other words of religion, as is fairly well known.[53] (*Secrets of Heaven* §1850:3, 4)

What we read here is that the true "Hebrew" church degenerated to a pseudo-church referred to as the "Jewish" one. Likewise the "Primitive" Christian church based upon the Lord's teachings degenerated to a pseudo-church, referred to as the Christian one. The general pattern is that charity and true faith get lost, and mere outward worship and a focus on doctrine divorced from charity take their place. The general process of the degeneration of churches is again taken up, in great detail, in §§2312–2468, referring to Genesis 19, and in §§2901–2986, referring to Genesis 23. From here on, Swedenborg continues discussing in general terms the nature and development of a true "spiritual" and "heavenly" church, sometimes also using the occasion to add further detail to his earlier description of specific churches (thus, for example, in the commentaries in §§4811–4930 on Genesis 38, which interprets Judah as meaning the "Jewish church," and Tamar as meaning the "genuine church"). These long exegetical chapters become increasingly technical, with much space devoted to detailed descriptions of questions such as, for example, "the union of earthly truth with spiritual virtue by various means" (§3902). We notice that, throughout all these discussions, the general framework remains the one described above, which links love to good and faith to truth, and subdivides love into spiritual and heavenly. One excellent further example of this approach (but many more could be given) is the commentary on Genesis 48 (§§6216–6306), which deals with "the church's intellect (consisting of truth) and its will (consisting of goodness). Ephraim means the church's intellect; Manasseh, its will" (§6216).

Genesis on the Lord's Inner Development

Swedenborg leaves no doubt that the members of the Jewish church had become focused on outward things so completely that they had entirely lost touch with internal verities and had become incapable of spiritual understanding (see also Hanegraaff 2004a). By the time this church had reached its final stages of decay, human consciousness had sunk to the lowest point in history; and it was at that point of deepest darkness that the Lord appeared on earth.

The chapters from Genesis 12 on are considered historically accurate, as we have seen, but their inner meaning is not about Abraham and his descendants but about the inner development of the Lord in his years of infancy, childhood, and boyhood. His inner development was one that led from a state of darkness to one of light, thus providing the ideal model of the development that each human individual should undergo. The ensuing interpretations do not, however, add up to a coherent account in temporal sequence: Swedenborg does not give us a coherent, sequential spiritual biography of the Lord's inner life. While the descriptions do convey a sense of how the Lord only gradually became aware of his true identity and his mission,[54] Swedenborg hardly presents this in a narrative form but mostly speaks in abstract terms about the various aspects of his spiritual maturation. For example, he points out that the phrase "Go from your land" means that the Lord was to withdraw from bodily and worldly concerns (*Secrets of Heaven* §1407); that "there was famine in the land" means the scarcity of knowledge that still affected him when he was young (§§1459–1460); that "Abraham went down into Egypt to reside as an immigrant" means that the Lord was taught concepts from the Word (§1461); that the wars described in Genesis 14 mean the spiritual battles he fought;[55] and so on. These discussions again tend to become quite technical, for example, when they deal with the precise processes by which the

Lord's human quality came to be joined to his divine quality (represented by Lot and Abraham, respectively);[56] by which his rational side came to fruition through "the influence of his inner self on his outer self's desire for information" (§1890); by which truth was connected with good within this rational side (§1898–1902); by which "the heavenly part of the spiritual dimension influenced and united with facts on the earthly level" (§5396b); and so on (§§3012–3212). Throughout, the discussions bear the imprint of Swedenborg's systematic scientific mind: the awakening to divine consciousness is described by means of a dry and precise technical language, reminiscent of physics or chemistry. It would be beyond the scope of this overview to analyze these discussions in detail: any value they may have for the reader lies not in the broad outlines of the message, as already sketched above, but in the specific details of Swedenborg's commentary on each and every verse.

Exodus on the Spiritual Church

The same is true for Swedenborg's interpretation of Exodus. If large parts of Genesis deal with the inner processes by means of which the Lord came to full spiritual consciousness, the whole of Exodus deals with the church that he founded. Again, the presentation is not in temporal sequence and takes the form of often highly abstract generalized statements. To get a sense of what this means, take the example of Exodus 1:1–6. The biblical text is given as follows (to clarify the relation with Swedenborg's interpretation, the passage has been subdivided by the present author into six numbered segments; these are different from the verse divisions):

> [1] And these are the names of the sons of Israel coming to Egypt with Jacob (a man and his household they came): [2] Reuben, Simeon, Levi, and Judah; Issachar, Zebulun, and Benjamin; Dan and Naphtali, Gad and Asher. [3] And every soul issuing from Jacob's thigh was seventy souls. [4] And Joseph was in Egypt. [5] And Joseph died, and all his brothers, and all that generation. [6] And the children of Israel reproduced and burgeoned, and multiplied and proliferated greatly, greatly, and the earth was filled with them. (*Secrets of Heaven* §6633)

In Swedenborg's reading this means:

> [1] The nature of the church after truth has been introduced into secular facts in regard to truth and goodness.
> [2] This whole process of the establishment of the church, from start to finish (the names of the twelve sons of Jacob and the tribes named after them meaning all aspects of goodness and truth, that is, of love and faith).
> [3] Everything produced by general truth, which was complete.
> [4] There was a heavenly quality within the earthly level.
> [5] The situation with the inner plane of the church had now changed, and likewise the situation with the outer plane in particular and general.
> [6] The church's truth grew in goodness; it grew tremendously in the truth that comes from goodness, until the church was full.[57]

The development of the "spiritual church" having been described in these highly abstract terms, its deliverance by the Lord begins to be described from Exodus 3 on: the members of the church are taught that the Lord will deliver them and "that he will take them to heaven after they have been given many different kinds of truth and goodness" (*Secrets of Heaven* §6825). Swedenborg continues to systematically apply this truth-good duality, for example, by asserting that Moses represents the goodness of divine law, and Aaron, its truth.[58]

Those who belonged to the true spiritual church were delivered, but those in the church who were governed by faith separated from charity— and therefore remained "steeped in falsity and evil"—underwent damnation. This process of damnation is the true meaning of the eleven[59] plagues of Egypt, each one of which is interpreted in great detail as representing a "stage of devastation." Swedenborg continues by interpreting the wanderings through the desert as the further preparation of those belonging to the spiritual church before the Lord's coming. In order for them to be led to heaven, they first had to be "conducted safely through the midst of damnation and then underwent spiritual challenges, the Lord always at their side" (§8039). This process, too, including all the struggles, is described in the greatest detail. In Exodus 19, we are told about "the Lord's revelation of divine truth from heaven" (§8748). The Ten Commandments given in Exodus 20 are interpreted in detail as "the divine truth that needs to be grafted onto virtue in people belonging to the Lord's spiritual church" (§8859). The laws, regulations, and punishments given from Exodus 21 on are obviously given a spiritual sense, as referring to offenses against the truth espoused by faith and the good embraced by charity, as well as "falsity . . . in doctrine, and evil . . . in life" (§9246). Having interpreted Exodus 24 as describing the essential nature of the Word (§9370), Swedenborg interprets the sanctuary and the ark of the covenant, as well as the various other technical descriptions beginning with Exodus 25, in a spiritual sense:

> The dwelling place would represent heaven itself; the ark in it, the deepest heaven; and the testimony or law in the ark, the Lord. The bread of faces on the table, and the lamp stand, would represent heavenly qualities received from the Lord in the heavens, and Aaron's garments would represent the spiritual qualities received from him there. (*Secrets of Heaven* §9455)[60]

The consecration of Aaron and his sons to the priesthood refers to the glorification of the Lord in his human incarnation, and Swedenborg then moves on to the Lord's establishment of a "representative church" among "people who do good out of love for and faith in the Lord," and the bond between the Lord and that church (§10326). The church could not be established among the Israelite people because they were wholly externally oriented and would only have profaned the holy things of heaven if these had been disclosed to them (see Hanegraaff 2004a). Exodus 35 is said to "summarize all the varieties of goodness and truth in the church and in heaven on which worship of the Lord is based" (§10725).

And then, quite surprisingly, Swedenborg suddenly gives up. The inner meaning of Exodus 36–40 is not explained because, as he states separately for each of these five chapters, everything in it can easily be deduced from what has been said previously.[61] In this manner, Swedenborg's extraordinarily detailed decoding of Genesis and Exodus comes to an incredibly abrupt end. After thousands of pages, the reader is preparing himself for some kind of grand finale; instead, the entire work ends without even a conclusion, as if interrupted in mid-thought. Referring to my earlier analogy, *Secrets of Heaven* ends like an "unfinished symphony."

5

Accounts of Memorable Occurrences

IN THIS CHAPTER, WE WILL FIRST GIVE A GENERAL OVERVIEW OF HOW Swedenborg looks at the nature and structure of heaven and hell and how he describes their inhabitants. Next, we will discuss his celebrated concept of the "universal human." Finally we will look at what he writes about hells and the process of spiritual devastation.

Heaven, Hell, and Their Inhabitants

While Swedenborg himself attached very great importance to his sentence-by-sentence exegesis of the Word, there can be no doubt that his eventual success as a religious author must be attributed, rather, to his visionary accounts of "things heard and seen" in heaven and hell. *Secrets of Heaven* originally does not seem to have attracted many readers,[62] and those that were interested tended to zoom in on the spectacular accounts of memorable occurrences (we will see that even a biblicist theologian like Friedrich Christoph Oetinger, with his great interest in questions of biblical exegesis, was no exception in this regard). Swedenborg appears to have realized at one point that, from what we would nowadays call a public relations perspective, the memorable occurrences were by far his strongest "selling point" and decided to adapt his publishing strategy. In 1758, that is, two years after the final volume of *Secrets of Heaven* was published, no fewer than five much smaller works appeared, four of which draw heavily on the non-exegetical parts of his magnum opus.[63] Two of them have their basis in what we have called the "first strand" of *Secrets of Heaven: De Nova Hierosolyma et Ejus Doctrina Coelesti* (The New Jerusalem and Its Heavenly Teaching) is dependent on the "Teachings about Charity" and "Teachings about Charity and Faith," and the contents of *De Equo Albo* (The White Horse) are largely drawn from *Secrets of Heaven* §§2760-2763. Most influential, however, became the two books which have their basis in the memorable occurrences: *De Telluribus in Mundo Nostro Solari* (known as "Other Planets") is an only slightly edited re-publication of the final parts of the "third strand"; and Swedenborg's most popular work, *De Coelo et Ejus Mirabilibus, et de Inferno* (Heaven and Its Wonders and Hell), is a much amplified and rearranged presentation of material found throughout the rest of the memorable occurrences.[64]

As pointed out by George F. Dole, Swedenborg was "clearly concerned to convey the connection between *Heaven and Hell* and *Secrets of Heaven*" (Dole 2000, 3). Not only were the contents of the smaller book referred to as "secrets of heaven" in §1, but *Heaven and Hell* is heavily annotated with cross-references to *Secrets of Heaven* (see Swedenborg 2000, 451–454). Dole draws the logical conclusion that

> Swedenborg intended *Heaven and Hell* at least in part as a vehicle for information already published in *Secrets of Heaven*. As well as demonstrating a striking concern for consistency, the cross-references clearly indicate a hope that it would attract the reader to that larger work. (Dole 2000, 4)

Indeed, with the exception of the final parts on the inhabitants of other planets, the memorable occurrences strand consists entirely of information about heaven and hell and their inhabitants. Swedenborg first speaks of what happens to people when they awake from death and enter into eternal life (§§168–189, 314–319, 320–323, 443–448), and continues with a general sketch of heaven and hell, as well as what may be seen—surprising in an author with a Lutheran background—as an equivalent of purgatory (§§449–459, 537–553, 684–700, 814–831, 938–970, 1106–1113). We will come back to this below. A short part is devoted to the present condition of the members of the earliest church (they are now very high up in heaven and live in a state of supreme happiness), as well as of their later descendants up to those who perished in the Flood and are now in one of the lowest hells (§§1114–1129, 1265–1272). The heavenly world of spirits and angels is described in rich detail at intervals throughout

§§1273–1885, which include long discussions of subjects such as the angels' and spirits' manner of perception (§§1383–1400, 1504–1520), their speech (§§1634–1650, 1757–1764), and how they understand the inner meaning of the Word (§§1767–1777, §§1869–1879). From here, Swedenborg moves to a series of specific subjects: the differences between, and heavenly origins of, visions, dreams, and prophecy (§§1966–1983); the Last Judgment, as actually referring not to an event on earth but to the after-death fate of the individual (§2117–2134); the state of children in the other life (§§2289–2309); the difference between outer memory, which belongs to the body, and inner memory, which belongs to the spirit (the latter constituting the individual's "Book of Life" in which everything he or she has ever thought, said, or done is written down up to the tiniest detail, and on the basis of which he or she is judged after death; §§2469–2494); the after-death fate of peoples and nations that were born outside the church (generally they are described much more mildly than the Jews and especially the Christians, most of whom are seen as much worse than the non-Christians §§2589–2605); how marriage and adultery are regarded in heaven (§§2727–2759);[66] and true human freedom as opposed to the pseudo-freedom that comes from hell (§§2870–2893).

Having discussed these specific aspects, Swedenborg returns to the general picture. He first provides a long theoretical discussion of what is meant by representations and correspondences (§§2987–3003, 3213–3227, 3337–3352, 3472–3485); and from that perspective he proceeds to a very detailed description of the structure of the heavenly "universal human," on which more below.[67] Finally, there are paragraphs about the nature of sicknesses (all of them have their origin in hell; §§5711–5727); the two angels, one spiritual and one heavenly, and the two infernal spirits—more precisely, an evil spirit and a genius, or demon—that are always present with, and fight over the soul of, each individual (see especially §§5977–5980); and the nature of the soul and the "inflow" of the divine into it.[68]

The Universal Human Constituted of Angelic Communities

If we take the accounts of memorable occurrences as a whole and try to combine their discussions about various aspects of heaven and hell into a coherent picture, we can draw some conclusions that are never made explicit by Swedenborg himself but are nevertheless implicit in his work. To begin with, Swedenborg states that "the whole of heaven has been formed to correspond with the Lord and his divine humanity. Human beings have been formed to correspond in absolutely every particular with heaven, and through heaven with the Lord" (*Secrets of Heaven* §3624). In other words, there are three levels: the Lord himself, his heavenly manifestation as a "universal human" of enormous proportions, and the human being as a small version of the universal human. About the Lord himself, as he exists in and of himself, Swedenborg says practically nothing; but the fact that the universal human "represents"[69] him means that the two cannot be conflated, and the same is implied by statements such as that the Lord appears as the sun to the inhabitants of heaven,[70] and that inhabitants of the third heaven "see the Lord himself" (§3475).

Much attention, in contrast, goes to the heavenly universal human. Universal it certainly is: "the Lord's heaven is immense—so immense as to surpass all belief. The inhabitants on our planet are very few, by comparison—almost like a pond in relation to the ocean" (§3631). Essential to Swedenborg's concept is that this entire heavenly universal human *consists of* spirits and angels, who are ordered in spiritual and angelic communities. In the long descriptions from §3624 to §5573, he discusses the anatomy of this universal human's body in meticulous detail, describing how every one of its organs is constituted of specific communities and sub-communities, the spiritual orientation of which corresponds to the inner sense of the components of human anatomy. One cannot but be reminded here of the detailed anatomical studies that had occupied Swedenborg in his scientific work during the years immediately preceding his spiritual crisis and the results of which were published in his *Oeconomia Regni Animalis* (Dynamics of the Soul's Domain; 1740–1741). In addition, several scholars have seen in Swedenborg's universal human a clear example of Kabbalistic influence as well. Usually, in this regard, they have referred to the figure of *Adam Kadmon*,[71] while seldom mentioning the equally obvious parallels in the *Schi'ur Koma* tradition about the measures of God's mystical body.[72] But given the absence in Swedenborg of any explicit references to Jewish sources in that regard, how convincing is it to explain his universal human as an instance of "borrowing"? Elsewhere it has been argued by the present author that we are dealing here with a case of phenomenological similarity, which is insufficient as proof of actual dependence (Hane-graaff 2004a). Anybody acquainted with the ancient idea that the human being is a microcosmos corresponding with the macrocosmos can draw the logical conclusion—without any need for Kabbalah—that, if a human being is a small world, the large world must look like a human being;[73] and Swedenborg himself quite explicitly refers to the concept of the macro-cosmos in discussing the universal human. In doing so, however, with char-acteristic attention to logical consistency and completeness, he distinguishes between the inner and the outer self, corresponding to the inner heaven and the outer cosmos:

> The inner self is made in the image of heaven, and the outer self, in the image of the world. In fact the inner self is heaven in *its* smallest form, while the outer self is the world in its smallest form, so that the person is a microcosm. (*Secrets of Heaven* §6057)

Thus, we see that the doctrine of the two worlds and the doctrine of macro-cosmos and microcosmos are combined, so as to yield a *double* picture: heaven relates to its individual inhabitant as a universal human to a small, and likewise the external physical universe relates to the individual living person as macrocosmos to microcosmos. The grand and the small mirror one another on a visible as well as an invisible, or outward and inward, level.

Now, this fundamental Swedenborgian concept appears to be insepa-rable from another basic assumption: his denial of any essential distinction between humans, spirits, angelic spirits, and angels, or put differently, his *radical humanization* of heaven (those of us who have lived the right kind of life become spirits, angelic spirits, and angels in the next life).[74] Swe-denborg's doctrines of the universal human and of the continuity from human beings to angels follow with strict logical necessity from only two axioms: (1) his firm belief in the difference between a higher and a lower world, and (2) his acceptance of the traditional notion of the human being as microcosmos. For an extremely systematic thinker like him, the combi-nation of the two inevitably brought up the question: if a human being is the universe in miniature, what then is a human being's parallel in heaven? Obviously, there were two candidates: angels and the spirits of the deceased. But since earth is modeled on heaven in all details, the existence of two kinds of microcosm in heaven would require two kinds in the material world as well, whereas we know that here on earth we have only human beings. Therefore, conceptual symmetry demanded that in heaven, too, there would be only *one* kind of entity; and since the existence of angels as well as the survival after death are attested by the Bible, logically the only remaining possibility is that angels are in fact none other than the spirits of the deceased.[75]

We begin to see how complex Swedenborg's concept of heaven really is, when we realize next that—in spite of his "enormous proportions"—the universal human in fact exists outside space and time:

> The form of heaven is astounding and completely outstrips any human ability to understand it, because it rises far above any ideas of form that we can possibly grasp by observing or even analyz-ing worldly forms. All heavenly communities are arranged in accord with that form, and strange to say, they revolve according to those forms, though angels and spirits do not sense the move-ment. It is like the daily course of the earth around its axis, or its annual course around the sun, which the inhabitants do not detect. . . .
>
> The forms that are still deeper (and more universal, too) are incomprehensible, . . . because the mere mention of forms brings with it the idea of space and time. On the deeper levels where heaven exists, no one perceives anything in terms of space or time—these being properties of the material world—but rather in terms of state and variations and changes of state. (*Secrets of Heaven* §§4041, 4043)[76]

It follows that, although spirits and angels experience concrete spatial envi-ronments—landscapes with woods, rivers, houses, and so forth—in which all kinds of things seem to happen to them in temporal sequence, all this is ultimately no more than a dreamlike illusion.[77] Spirits and angels in fact never go anywhere at all:

> all communities in the other world . . . maintain their own con-stant position in relation to the Lord, who appears to the whole

of heaven as the sun. What is surprising—and hardly any will believe it, since they cannot understand it—is that the communities there maintain this same position in relation to *everyone* there. No matter where you are, which way you turn, or how you move around, communities that appear on your right are always on your right, and those on your left are always on your left, even when you turn your face or move your body from quarter to quarter. . . .

Everyone . . . appears upright, head above and feet below. . . . Those in heaven have their heads toward the Lord. . . . The hellish, on the other hand, appear in angels' eyes with their head down and their feet up. (*Secrets of Heaven* §§3638, 3641)[78]

It is not too difficult for the reader to imagine that souls might subjectively experience a life in heavenly time and space, even though they are actually "fixed" in a certain position in the body of the universal human; for, after all, we all know how we can travel in our dreams while actually remaining in bed. But how a soul can possibly be "fixed" in any location at all, if there is no space to begin with, remains truly impossible to understand. One is not surprised, therefore, to find that Swedenborg—who is elsewhere always concerned with rationality and logical consistency—emphasizes in the strongest possible terms that *these* marvels are simply beyond human intelligence.

Hells and the Process of Spiritual Devastation

Having discussed these distinctions between the Lord himself, the universal human as his heavenly representation, and heaven as perceived from the perspective of its inhabitants, it remains to discuss briefly the two other environments in which human beings may find themselves after death: hell and "the place of spiritual devastations."

About hell we can be short. Just like heaven, it consists of innumerable communities (referred to as specific "hells," some of which are described in detail). They all exist outside the universal human "on different levels in all directions under the sole of the foot" (*Secrets of Heaven* §3640) and apparently in an upside-down position. This is enough, of course, to suggest that all the hells together must surely form some grand being in human form, just like the heavenly communities do. Interestingly, however, Swedenborg does *not* actually say so in *Secrets of Heaven*, although he does draw that conclusion in *Heaven and Hell*.[79] There is reason to assume that this reflects a certain amount of hesitation on Swedenborg's part concerning a subject on which he held somewhat conflicting ideas. If the heavenly universal human represents the Lord, it is logical to conclude that such an infernal grand being must represent his counterpart, the Devil; but this would seem to give the Devil a status precisely equal to that of the Lord, which has far-reaching and troubling theological implications. In *Secrets of Heaven*, at least, Swedenborg seems determined not to take that road: "It is wrong to believe that any devil has existed from the beginning of creation other than those who once were people" (§968).[80] When he nevertheless described hell as a grand being in his later writings, speaking of it as "a single devil", he would seem to have chosen the other way out of the dilemma. Whether this is correct, and if so, how he then dealt with the inevitable theological implications would merit a separate discussion beyond the scope of the present one, which must restrict itself to *Secrets of Heaven*.

Swedenborg is equally evasive about a final aspect of the afterlife that sits somewhat uneasily with the sharp ethical dualism of his system. Again and again, he makes clear that there is no such thing as a gray area between heaven and hell: those whose life is ruled by love for one's neighbor and for the Lord go to heaven, while those whose life is ruled by self-love and love for the world go to hell.[81] There is nothing in between. And yet, he does speak of an after-death state that allows human beings to be purged of their "falsity" so as to be eventually admitted to heaven. People who absorbed such falsity "out of simplicity and ignorance" spend a considerable length of time "in the underworld" (located "under the feet [of the universal human] and the region round about for a short distance"), where they undergo the process of devastation before finally being carried into heaven.[82] Clearly, this aspect of Swedenborg's teaching is reminiscent of what is known in Roman Catholicism as purgatory, a concept that was rejected by the Reformation and appears in a Lutheran context only rarely, and in a later period.[83]

PART TWO

Oetinger, Kant, and the Early
Reception of *Secrets of Heaven*

✣ 6 ✣

The Early Reception of *Secrets of Heaven*

A GENERAL RECEPTION HISTORY OF SWEDENBORG'S THOUGHT FALLS beyond the scope of this short book. Much has been written about his influence on later generations, including great names like William Blake (1757–1827), Friedrich Wilhelm Joseph von Schelling (1775–1854), Johann Wolfgang von Goethe (1749–1832), Johann Caspar Lavater (1741–1801), Honoré de Balzac (1799–1850), Fjodor Michailowitsch Dostojewski (1821–1881), Charles Baudelaire (1821–1867), August Strindberg (1849–1912), Ralph Waldo Emerson (1803–1882), Helen Keller (1880–1968), Arnold Schönberg (1874–1951), and Jorge Luis Borges (1899–1986).[84] While the importance of Swedenborgian concepts for these and many other writers, poets, artists, musicians, and philosophers is not in doubt, it is much more difficult to assess the importance of *Secrets of Heaven* specifically. After all, many of the ideas that we find in it can be found in other and later works by Swedenborg as well, and unless an author is explicit about his sources or gives precise quotations, one often cannot know exactly what he or she has read. This problem is greatly aggravated by the fact that, as we have seen, several of Swedenborg's most popular later writings are, in fact, re-edited versions of materials from *Secrets of Heaven*: when an author appears to be influenced by his ideas about heaven and hell or the inhabitants of other planets, he may as well have found them in those later publications rather than in *Secrets of Heaven* itself. To make matters worse, the further we move forward in history, away from Swedenborg's own time, the more we have to reckon with indirect transmission of his ideas: frequently people seem to have picked up some of his ideas from second-hand and not necessarily accurate accounts, and relatively few non-members of the New Church may have taken the trouble actually to read Swedenborg's works (cf. Wilkinson 1996, 19). Among those who did, many dipped into them rather than reading them from cover to cover; and for many such readers, the shorter books were no doubt more convenient than the massive and forbidding *Secrets of Heaven*. And finally, among those who did read the latter, one may well wonder how many took the trouble to read the theoretical and exegetical parts: here, too, the "accounts of memorable occurrences" were no doubt most attractive to most readers.

Given these problems, a reception history of *Secrets of Heaven* must be subject to a number of restrictions. First, the emphasis must be on the earliest period: immediately after the work was published, while Swedenborg's later writings were not yet available or not yet widely known. And second, the emphasis must be on authors who did more than merely pick up some of Swedenborg's ideas but made a serious attempt—on the basis specifically of *Secrets of Heaven*—at critically evaluating his perspective as a whole. The reception of *Secrets of Heaven* in later periods can certainly be traced to some extent—and a few examples will be discussed below; but although we know about a number of important authors who read Swedenborg's *magnum opus*, they usually read other works as well, and as a result, they become examples of the reception history of Swedenborg generally rather than of *Secrets of Heaven* specifically.

Now, if one applies these two guidelines, one finds the domain restricted immediately to the German context. Here Swedenborg found his most important commentators and critics as early as during his own lifetime, in the persons of Johann August Ernesti, and most notably, Friedrich Christoph Oetinger and Immanuel Kant. The considerable early interest in Swedenborg among German intellectuals[85] had much to do with Oetinger's translation of excerpts from *Secrets of Heaven*, published as early as 1765: it is this translation, rather than Swedenborg's original, on which most of them appear to have depended.[86] In France *Secrets of Heaven*'s reception history begins considerably later, mainly due to the fact that French translations do not seem to have become available before 1841.[87] An English translation of *Secrets of Heaven*, volume II, by John Marchant (d. 1769), was published simultaneously with the first Latin edition, in 1750; but this translation is extremely rare, and only two copies of it seem to survive (Tafel 1890, III, 974; Hyde 1906, 139). The complete *Secrets of*

Heaven, translated by John Clowes (1743–1841), first appeared in English in twelve volumes from 1783–1806; but when the first volume appeared, *Heaven and Hell* had already been available for five years (1778), in a translation by William Cookworthy (1705–1780) and Thomas Hartley (1709–1784), and various other works by Swedenborg had become available by 1806.[88] As for Swedenborg's home country, a "Philanthropic and Exegetic Society" devoted to publication and translation of his works existed for a few years (1786–1789) but managed only to get a few small parts into print; publication of Swedenborg's works long remained impossible due to suppression by the ecclestiastical and secular authorities.[89] *Secrets of Heaven* began to be published in Swedish translations only from 1821 on (see Hyde 1906, 190–194).

We will, therefore, concentrate most of our attention on the early reception, in Germany, by Johann August Ernesti and, especially, Friedrich Christoph Oetinger and Immanuel Kant. As will be seen, their attempts to come to terms with Swedenborg's *Secrets of Heaven* make for a fascinating story that deserves to be treated in some detail.

The very earliest review of *Secrets of Heaven* appeared in a German periodical, *Neue Zeitungen von Gelehrten Sachen*, in 1750. The anonymous author reports about new books that have recently appeared in London and makes the following, quite amazing remarks:

> Here [in London] one sees the following work, which was printed without mention of place of publication and author; *Arcana coelestia* [the complete latin title follows]. If the readers look through it only a little bit, they will quickly discover that, without doubt, the work was written by some pious person from among the blackcoats [*aus dem Pabstthum*; that is to say, a Roman Catholic], who has written it in a state of trance. It is really an anagogic or mystical explanation of the first 15 chapters of the first book of Moses. The author calls that the internal understanding of Scripture, which so far no man has known but which has been revealed to him; with the exception of what God has explained to the apostles, that is to say, for example, that sacrifices mean the Lord, or that the promised land Canaan and the city of Jerusalem mean heaven. But one should know, writes the author, that all special

things have an inner meaning, and refer to heaven, the church, faith, and what belongs to faith; since the external letter refers only to the Jewish church. At the end of the work we also see that these explanations have been made known to the author by means of visions, which are called living experience.

The review proceeds to give a generally correct sketch of some of the contents of Swedenborg's "memorable occurrences," and then comes to a conclusion. Swedenborg's scriptural exegesis is

> ... full of scholastic errors, and therefore should not be made further known by us here. The entire book belongs in the centuries of scholasticism, when people tormented their senses with such futile thoughts, while neglecting the truth of Scripture. It is not easy to believe that any person in his right mind would accept such mystical things as truths, or would believe that the unknown author has really been in the company of spirits, since it is easy to see that his overheated imagination has suggested to him such appearances, which might also fool other people who follow the disordered imagination, so that they do not know themselves what they think. Still, for pious weirdoes [*Grillenfänger*] and loafers this work may be a good pastime.[90]

So this staunch Protestant reviewer perceived in Swedenborg a Roman Catholic author! Bizarre though it may look to us, if we recall the discussion above about the Protestant rejection of allegorical exegesis (chapter 3), this misinterpretation is understandable enough.

Much better known is the review published in 1760 by the influential philologist and theologian Johann August Ernesti, who likewise did not have much positive to say about *Secrets of Heaven*.[91] Like the earlier anonymous reviewer, Ernesti emphasizes the "mystical or allegorical" nature of Swedenborg's exegetical method, discussing Swedenborg's interpretation of Genesis 1 as a sample. His visionary accounts he finds "so confused and obscure that one sees that he had not yet been right in his mind. . . ."[92] The conclusion leaves no doubt about Ernesti's opinion:

One sees without difficulty that, under this fanatical form, the author wishes to bring forward materialism and his own philosophical opinions, and that this is a novel of a new kind which may perhaps be compared with Klimm's subterraneum journey,[93] except that the latter fiction is harmless, while the former in its misuse and distortion of Holy Writ, under the guise of the above mentioned inner sense, is highly worthy of punishment. For the rest, we have no fear that many people will read the book or allow themselves to be seduced by it. Yet, sad to say, many people are commencing to take pleasure in such dreams.[94]

The most interesting point of Ernesti's remarks is his interpretation of *Secrets of Heaven* as presenting an implicitly materialist worldview. It is not entirely clear whether at the time of writing Ernesti was already aware of the identity of the author.[95] If not, his remark must be seen as rather perceptive, in that he seems to recognize *Secrets of Heaven* as written by a scientist trained in the new natural philosophy.

Ernesti repeated the same point seven years later, in a review of Heinrich Wilhelm Clemm's *Vollständige Einleitung in die Religion und Gesammte Theologie* (Complete Introduction to Religion and the Whole of Theology, 1767). In response to the controversy created by Oetinger's translations from *Secrets of Heaven* and Kant's *Träume eines Geistersehers*, both of which had come out recently, Clemm (1725–1775) had written a rather lengthy excursus devoted to Swedenborg. He argued that it is not possible for us to decide whether Swedenborg's visions are mere phantasies, whether they have been inspired by an evil spirit, or whether they are true. Since we cannot know which of these three explanations is correct, we should pronounce a *non liquet*: "case still undecided" (Clemm 1767, 204–217). Ernesti did not agree:

From Swedenborg's writings and the excerpts we have given therefrom, it is clear that, like the crude Fanatici, he is a naturalist, and that he hides his naturalism under cover of Biblical expressions, or changes the Biblical theology into a *naturalismum* as, in a different way, do the Socinians. And that is the key to

the whole matter. In addition to the three possibilities which the
Herr. Dr. [Clemm] lays down . . . there is a fourth which without doubt is the right one. They could be fictitious inventions
wherewith he desires to deceive the world; and in his heart he
may laugh at the people (as also they deserve), who believe him
and do not understand his artfulness.[96]

This passage was copied in a book published in 1771 by J. C. Cuno
(1707–1796) (Paulus ab Indagine), based upon the latter's discussions with
Swedenborg in Amsterdam (see Anonymus [J. C. Cuno] 1771, 9–10). Having received a copy from the author, Swedenborg was understandably upset
at seeing himself branded a deliberate fraud and wrote a note to Cuno in
which he called Ernesti's attack "against the laws of honour." He deemed
it unworthy to respond in like manner but made a reference to a passage
in his *Vera Christiana Religio* as being relevant to the matter. When Cuno—
who was quite critical towards Swedenborg and considered his writings
theologically suspect (see, for example, Anonymus [J.C. Cuno] 1771, 6,
10)—refused to circulate the note further, he sent copies to his correspon-
dents Gabriel Beyer and Friedrich Christoph Oetinger, who published it
in one of his collections. We learn from it that one of the "Memorable
Occurrences" in *Vera Christiana Religio* is indeed written against Ernesti.

Swedenborg had told Cuno that he had met Ernesti's *spiritus familiaris*
in the spiritual world and had debated with him.[97] We find the debate in
Vera Christiana Religio §137. It is a fascinating piece that must be read in
its entirety to be appreciated. A synod is held in heaven, with the ante-
Nicene apostolic fathers seated on the right and the modern adherents of
"justification by faith alone" on the left. A man presiding over the meeting thunders against a new heretic who, although a layman without for-
mal theological training, dares to reject the doctrine of the trinity and has
"transferred faith to the second person"—worse, to the second person in
his human form. From this, he asks the assembly, "What else can result
but a faith from which materialism flows as from a fountain?" The heretic
referred to is, of course, no other than Swedenborg himself. However, one
of the ante-Nicene fathers, who turns out to be an angel, criticizes the president's perspective and takes Swedenborg's side. A bit later on, Swedenborg asks the president "with whom he is associated" (that is to say, of

what person on earth he is the *spiritus familiaris*). The spirit answers that he is associated with a celebrated man of the church, who lives "not far from the tomb of Luther." This confirms what we already suspected: he represents Ernesti, who lives in Leipzig, not far from Luther's tomb in Wittenberg. The spirit is then solemnly admonished to try and make Ernesti change his mind: it is he, and not Swedenborg, who allows his pen "to plough a furrow" in which the thoughtless may sow materialism. The spirit objects; but, in the debate that follows, he is eventually silenced by Swedenborg's evidently superior theology. And thus it was that Swedenborg, unable to silence Ernesti on earth, at least gained a victory over him in heaven.

7

Friedrich Christoph Oetinger

FRIEDRICH CHRISTOPH OETINGER IS CONSIDERED THE FOREMOST representative of Christian theosophy in the eighteenth century.[98] After studies of liberal arts and theology in Tübingen and a series of educational travels, he held appointments as a pastor in various smaller German towns. In 1752, he was promoted to the office of superintendent (dean) in Weinsberg, where he got into problems with his community, partly due to his "abstruse" sermons. After a period as superintendent in Herrenberg, in 1765 he was appointed ducal councillor, prelate, and abbot in Murrhardt, where he took over duties in 1766. By that time, he had already written some of his most important works. Of particular and lasting importance to Oetinger were the writings of Jacob Böhme, which he had begun to read around 1725 at the instigation of a powder maker in Tübingen, Johann Caspar Obenberger. Böhme would remain central to Oetinger's thinking throughout his life, as will be seen. By the end of the 1720s, Oetinger also came into contact with the Christian Kabbalah, in the form of Christian Knorr von Rosenroth's (1636–1689) *Kabbala denudata* and personal acquaintance with the Frankfurt kabbalist Koppel Hecht (d. 1729), who called his attention to the similarities between Böhme and the Kabbalah. Oetinger continued to deepen his knowledge of Jewish mysticism thereafter, becoming particularly influenced by the Lurianic Kabbalah. Throughout his later life, Oetinger would defend and develop a Böhmian-kabbalistic theosophy, integrated with a biblical literalism in the Pietist tradition of Johann Albrecht Bengel (1687–1752), opposing it against the hated rationalism and philosophical idealism of Gottfried Leibniz and Christian Wolff.[99]

Oetinger's First Acquaintance with Swedenborg

The most important fruit of Oetinger's Christian-kabbalistic interests appeared in 1763, under the title *Offentliches Denckmahl der Lehr-Tafel einer weyl. Würtembergischen Princessin Antonia* (Public Monument of the Educational Tableau of a [the] late Württembergian Princess Antonia)[100]: a commentary on a rich emblematic painting from 1663, commissioned by Antonia princess of Württemberg (1613–1679) and donated by her in 1673 to the church in Bad Teinach, where it has remained to the present day. Integrated in the chaotic structure of this work—Oetinger is an extremely careless and unsystematic writer—one finds not only discussions of Böhme and the Kabbalah but also of the natural sciences and philosophy. The authors specifically discussed in the *Lehrtafel* are Böhme, Newton, Malebranche, Leibniz, Wolff, Zinzendorf, Spener, Frederick the Great—and Emanuel Swedenborg. The short section on "The Swedenborgian System" consists of a summary in sixteen points, based upon the *Principia rerum naturalium* (1734) and amounts to Oetinger's first attempt at a comparison between Swedenborg and Böhme. He apparently does not know what to make of Swedenborg's system of natural philosophy: it is so clearly mechanical, and yet . . .

> 6. The soul is similar to a clockwork, according to Schwedenborg's doctrine, but its wheels are *Spirit and Life*. . . .
> 9. According to Schwedenborg there is a circular movement in the soul, and it is likewise according to Jac. Böhmen. . . .
> 11. Schwedenborg does not give sufficient attention to the sources of autonomous movement [*Selbst-Bewegungs-Quellen*].
> 12. And yet to some extent he corresponds with Jac. Böhmen's three principles. . . .
> 15. With Schwedenborg everything is in an order of succession [*hinter einander*], with Jac. Böhm [it is] integrated [*in einander*]. (Oetinger [1763] 1977, I, 153)

Faced with such contradictions, Oetinger concludes with an appeal to eclecticism characteristic of his own outlook as well as of the *vernünftige Hermetik* (Enlightened Hermeticism) of his times:[101]

16. Pious scholars should well *investigate everything and keep what is good*. (Oetinger [1763] 1977, I, 153)

Two years later, in 1765, Oetinger completed his most important theological work, the *Theologia ex idea vitae deducta*;[102] and in the same year he also read Swedenborg's *Secrets of Heaven*. He now discovered to his astonishment that the person he knew as a natural scientist of the mechanical school had become a writer of visionary works; and again his reaction is quite ambiguous:

> From being the greatest philosopher, he [Swedenborg] has become a small apostle. . . . The book is called "Heavenly secrets. . . ." [It] is in Latin in large quarto volumes. . . . It contains miracles: amazing, unheard-of, important things. His experiences are beautiful, but his scriptural explanations are ex uno visu [one-sided]. Nothing [of that] flusters me, I can combine everything, I'm not a theologian of only a single direction [*ich bin kein Theologe von einem einzigen Leist*]. But, oh, what a book is this! Krafft says that the descriptions are so detailed that he believes it is better to go over [into eternity] in faith alone than with such detailed information.[103]

In a nutshell, this letter contains the core problems that would remain central to Oetinger's debate with Swedenborg in the years to come. It clearly shows that, from the very outset, he drew a distinction between Swedenborg's scriptural exegesis on the one hand, and his visionary experiences, on the other. The former he finds wanting, for reasons we will explore below, but he cannot help being impressed by the latter.

Swedenborg's and Others' Earthly and Heavenly Philosophy

In the same year 1765 appeared Oetinger's *Swedenborgs und anderer Irrdische und himmlische Philosophie* (Swedenborg's and Others' Earthly and Heavenly Philosophy), which marks the beginning of a series of writings that document the development of his struggle with the Swedish seer.[104] Oetinger's goal is to prove the truth of Holy Scripture on the basis not only of the *sensus communis* (the understanding shared by the community of Christians) but also of modern philosophy. He attempts to find a "third way" that will avoid both the idealism of Leibniz and Wolff and the alternative of materialism, represented for him by Giorgio Baglivi (1668–1707). According to the book's original conception, the foundations for such a higher synthesis could be found in the writings of Jacob Böhme. The very title of the published version alone would, however, seem to suggest that, while the book was being written, the newly discovered visionary Swedenborg came to gain precedence over Böhme. I will argue that this is correct to some extent, but not at all in the measure suggested by Ernst Benz in his foundational study of the subject (Benz 1947, ch. III).

As Benz demonstrated, the different parts of Oetinger's book did not emerge in the order suggested by the final published version. The earliest part is volume II, sections B–H; these are entirely focused on Böhme, whose perspective is compared with the systems of Nicolas Malebranche, Isaac Newton, Detlev Cluver, Christian Wolff, Wilhelm Gottfried Ploucquet, Giorgio Baglivi, and Johann Ludwig Fricker. In terms of content and structure, it is close to the similar comparisons found in the *Lehrtafel*. Next, having discovered Swedenborg's *Secrets of Heaven*, Oetinger seems immediately to have begun translating large parts of the "accounts of memorable occurrences" into German, and this became volume I, sections B–C, called "Swedenborg's Heavenly Philosophy."[105] They are followed by a commentary (volume I, section D). Only after having finished these translations and this commentary did Oetinger write what became the book's first section (volume I, section A), on "The System of Swedenborg's Earthly Philosophy." It is important to realize that, in this period of his life, Oetinger was gravely ill and believed to be on his deathbed; under these circumstances, he relied for his discussion on old notes about Swedenborg's *Principia rerum naturalium*, which he had read around 1735. Finally, having miraculously recovered, he undertook a new study of the *Principia*; and this resulted in the section "Further Implications of Swedenborg's Earthly Philosophy," published as volume II, section A.

Oetinger's first discussion of Swedenborg, therefore, appears in volume I, section D, and, as will be seen, it is highly significant in view of later developments. Oetinger immediately begins by attacking the allegorical approach to scriptural exegesis, which at the time was gaining prominence in a context of philosophical idealism, in favor of a literalist, concrete and corporeal understanding of scripture in line with Oetinger's central concept of *Geistleiblichkeit* (on which more below):

> He who reads the Holy Scripture, not fuddled by philosophical ideas but like a child, without prejudices, sees right away that God . . . is presented as riding the wings of the wind; that the angels and spirits are painted as extended *spiracula* or winds and fiery flames; that man has received the breath of life immediately from God's mouth; . . . that the spirits after death, when the body lies in the grave, really have eyes, ears, tongues and suchlike; in short, that the joys of heaven are described in no other way than in living, spiritual-bodily extensions *[geistlich körperlichen Ausdehnungen]*, not as dead material figures.
>
> The learned find this all too imaginative. They wish to clean these rough concepts from all bodily indecency, so that finally everything comes down to a mere unknowable I-don't-know-what *[ein blosses incogitables weiss nicht was]*. This is the foundation of this world's unbelief. But those who read the Holy Scripture in such a way that they allow their thought to be built from the clearly expressed Word, do exactly the opposite. They understand it the way it lies before us . . . because the clear Word already provides enough of the basic concepts of the Men of God. . . . There is grace and peace in their heart, while a thousand unrests and a thousands doubts are in the hearts of the philosophical exegetes of Scripture. (Oetinger [1765] 1977, I, 120–121)

In his defense of what has often been called a "massive biblical literalism," Oetinger was and would always remain the faithful pupil of the great Pietist theologian Johann Albrecht Bengel (1687–1752; see Mälzel 1970; Brecht 1995, esp. 251–259). In 1765, he was apparently convinced that he had found in Swedenborg a powerful ally and witness against the allegorical exegesis favored by the idealists in the tradition of Leibniz and Wolff: now, he writes, a great philosopher appears on the stage, who tells us that things are exactly how Scripture tells us they are, instead of evaporating Scripture into empty abstractions. A bit later on, Oetinger says that the

Bible shows "that everything spiritual is covered with a heavenly extension and an indestructible bodiliness [*Leiblichkeit*]," as he has himself demonstrated in his *Theologia* and his *Lehrtafel*. These "ultimate concepts," he claims, "which I have proved from the Holy Scripture, are also Schwedenborg's ultimate concepts" (Oetinger [1765] 1977, I, 128. Cf. also o.c., 133–134).

We will see that Oetinger was mistaken about Swedenborg intentions, due to a fundamental tension between the latter's method of exegesis and the contents of his visions. Concerning the rest of the section, it must be noted that, in spite of the above, Oetinger is nothing if not critical about Swedenborg. His philosophy he finds too mechanical and hard to reconcile with the implications of his visionary experiences; when Swedenborg writes about the elements, he clearly cannot match the profundity of Böhme; and while he may have much to say about spirits and angels, his vision remains limited to that domain only. Implicitly Oetinger criticizes Swedenborg's belief in a continuity between men and angels, by pointing out that the angels do not participate in salvation through the flesh and blood of Christ: "For the angels are of another subordination. Human beings are covered with the elements of the water, blood and spirit of Jesus, and seem to represent a wholly different order, by means of which God wishes to show the angels something they do not know" (Oetinger [1765] 1977, I, 135).

More such critical notes are to be found in the two discussions of Swedenborg's "earthly philosophy," where Böhme consistently emerges victorious from any direct comparison between the two. On page two, Oetinger already points out that Swedenborg's mechanical philosophy, which claims that all movement is spiral and comes from one and the same source, cannot account for the "movement" of the perverted will that results in sin and evil. Oetinger concludes by rejecting Swedenborg's dualism in favor of Böhme's panentheism,[106] correctly pointing out that the former leaves no room for the basic Böhmian concept of a fall and reintegration of nature:

1. The Swedenborgian system is too much outside of God. According to Holy Scripture, God is above all, through all, and in all; God is not τo παν, but all in all. Therefore one should not put the universe so far outside of God as the earth is from heaven.

The universe is in God. God is its centre, but not *physicum*; he does not belong to the birth of nature, but remains and resides within himself, even though he everywhere permeates nature. God is autonomous; nature is not.

2. The Swedenborgian system does not suffice in order to explain the fall of nature. Here all philosophical systems fall silent: only Jacob Böhm's system manages to make the fall and the reintegration understandable. The central concept in Jac. Böhm's system is the one that is absent with all the philosophers, namely, the *ens penetrabile*, which is neither material nor purely spiritual, but indifferent to spirit and to matter.[107]

Essentially the same pattern is continued in volume II: Oetinger affirms that Swedenborg's philosophy "makes more sense than all philosophies," but that he cannot match the profundity of Böhme. This is further demonstrated by the examples of humanity's salvation through the death of Christ, the Böhmian doctrine of the seven spirits, the fall of man, and the emergence of new worlds (Oetinger [1765] 1977, II, 170–172). What Böhme and Swedenborg have in common is the fact that they are neither naturalists nor deists and that they give convincing explanations of the "births of things"; in any case, they are both to be preferred to the systems of Leibniz, Wolff, and Descartes.

Ernst Benz overstated his case by claiming that Oetinger had become "a convinced Swedenborgian" and "a tireless defender of Swedenborg" (Benz 1947, 35–36). Oetinger was certainly fascinated by the Swedish seer; but from the outset, he took a critical and eclectic approach to Swedenborg's teachings, and every comparison with Böhme fell out in favor of the latter. Without any doubt—and this is stated by Benz as well—what specifically attracted Oetinger in *Secrets of Heaven* was not Swedenborg's scriptural exegesis but his descriptions of "memorabilia" based upon spiritual vision.

Oetinger's book attracted wide attention and must be considered crucial to the subsequent spread of Swedenborg's fame in Germany. It also caused a direct conflict with the church authorities: in the wake of a viciously negative (and probably "arranged") review in the *Göttinger Anzeigen von gelehrten Sachen* (26/27, 1766, 201ff), the book was confiscated as "an offense against religion and theology" and its author received an official publication ban.[108] It seems clear that the authorities hardly bothered to differentiate between Böhme and Swedenborg or to recognize Oetinger's criticism of the latter. In any case, from this moment on, Oetinger was forced to take recourse to various tricks and devices to have his works published; and during the next years, he waged a continuous but unsuccessful battle to defend himself against the accusations and have the ban lifted. The details of this development fall beyond the scope of our discussion and are readily available in Benz's standard work. Here I will concentrate on the main stages in the post-1765 development, insofar as they are necessary for understanding the essence of what was at stake between the Swabian and the Swedish theosopher.

From Qualified Acceptance to Unqualified Rejection

On October 13, 1765, Oetinger wrote a letter to Swedenborg, followed by a second one when he received no response. Swedenborg found both letters when he returned from Amsterdam and responded right away. This was the beginning of a correspondence that would continue until shortly before Swedenborg's death. Already in his first letter, Swedenborg significantly remarks that, without divine revelation, not the least verse in the Bible (he is referring specifically to Revelation) can be understood. We have seen that this point is also made in the very first lines of *Secrets of Heaven* and is constantly repeated in later sections. Swedenborg finds it important to point out in his first letter to Oetinger that his writings should not be understood as "prophecies" but as "revelations." Prophecies in his view use unclear hieroglyphic, allegorical, symbolic, and imaginative language. Swedenborg, however, explains and reveals in clear and unambiguous language the true meaning of such mysterious statements; and he is able to do so only because the Lord himself has revealed to him their true meaning. The reference is, of course, to what we have described earlier as an allegorical method of "decoding" the literal sense so as to disclose the internal.

Nothing could be further from Oetinger's biblical literalism in the tradition of Bengel, and one can only be surprised at how long it actually took Oetinger to face up to this fact. Most likely the explanation has to do with a remarkable tension—perhaps a contradiction—that exists between

Swedenborg's method of exegesis and his visions. As formulated by Benz, at this point "[Oetinger] does not yet manage to get beyond the contradiction that Swedenborg's visions reveal heavenly realities whereas his exegesis of Scripture causes these realities to evaporate into abstract allegories" (Benz 1947, 80).[109]

I would suggest that Oetinger and Swedenborg did not essentially disagree about the nature of the spiritual world: both describe it in highly literal terms as filled with concrete and manifest realities. Their disagreement concerned the question of whether the spiritual realities manifest themselves *in this world*, literally as described in the Bible. Here Swedenborg maintained a strict Cartesian dualism. The material world is entirely "disenchanted," ruled by mechanical laws, and explicitly described as "dead."[110] It is not permeated by any divine principle or life-force, and it maintains no causal connections—either instrumental or occult[111]—with the spiritual world. The classic Cartesian problem of how, then, to explain that there can be any relation between these two worlds, Swedenborg solves in terms of his doctrine of correspondences, which, as we have seen, in his work has essentially the function of a scientific hypothesis. Clearly such a framework makes it impossible to imagine the spiritual manifesting itself in concrete and bodily fashion in our material world.[112]

Oetinger's philosophy of nature, in contrast, was thoroughly panentheist and predicated on the unquestionable authority of the Bible, according to the Protestant perspective discussed earlier. Human beings cannot presume to set the rules and define the criteria according to which the Bible should be read and interpreted, for this would mean that the frail and imperfect human understanding is given preference over God's perspective and is given the authority to decide what in the Bible is acceptable and what is not. God's Word itself is the authority: if we find its literal meaning hard to understand or accept, this is due to our imperfect perception and understanding rather than to any ambiguity or contradiction in the Bible. Neither can there be any contradiction between the Bible and the book of nature;[113] but one should realize that the natural world in its present fallen state is merely a "first draft" (*nur eine anfängliche Präparation, eine ébauche, ein bloser Entwurf* [H.I. Oetinger 1771, 22]) for a more perfect future world and still contains many "irregularities." For this reason, we cannot trust any formulation of universal "laws of nature": all we have is the necessarily fragmentary and provisory data of empirical research, and hence we cannot blindly trust even the signatures of things:

> Therefore there must as yet be much imperfection also with the *signatura rerum*.[114] . . . [T]he earth, as a planet, must change into a comet. But when according to the Creator's arbitrary revelation the earth is, still prior to the great separation of the idle and the truthful, brought to a state of regularity by means of a small adaptation of the polar star, so that the *Ecliptica* is brought nearer to the *Aequatori*, only at that moment will the *signatura rerum* attain their perfect state, the mountains will proclaim peace, and the hills justice, Ps. 72, 3. Truth will grow from the earth, Ps. 85, 12. The clouds will rain justice, and the earth will open up and bring only salvation, all this according to the *litera*. Then, then, will we perceive the *signaturas rerum* with our very eyes, without many reasonings, Jes. 52, 8, 9, 10. . . . Until that time, we *medici* must be content with reading a few grains of wisdom *per signaturas naturalis*. . . .[115]

This dynamic theosophical perspective on nature, as fallen and in need of regeneration, is alien to Swedenborg's Cartesian view of nature as a dead mechanism that can be grasped in terms of universal scientific laws; and this opposition is inseparable from the one that exists between Oetinger's incarnational theology, on the one hand, and Swedenborg's docetist tendencies on the other.[116]

Of crucial importance in this respect is Oetinger's key term *Geistleib-lichkeit*,[117] which unfortunately is almost untranslatable into English. It could be rendered rather clumsily as "spiritual bodiliness," but while Oetinger distinguishes between *Leib* and *Körper*, in English we have only the term *body* for both. *Körper* in Oetinger's terminology stands for the gross body in its present fallen state;[118] *Leib*, however, is an extremely positive term (and it is because of this difference that the translation "spiritual corporeality" might be seen as somewhat misleading). The background to this valuation is to be sought in the incarnational theosophy of Jacob Böhme, whose system describes how the unmanifested *Ungrund* gives birth to God and refers to God's body as "eternal nature" (*die ewige Natur*).[119]

More specifically, in Oetinger's theosophy the incarnation of God does not only refer to the birth of Jesus Christ but can be traced at least as far back as the appearance of Wisdom or the world soul, whose body of light constitutes the angelic heaven (Deghaye 2000, 169 and *passim*). All these instances of incarnation—the birth of God himself, the appearance of Wisdom, the birth of Jesus Christ—are to be seen as models for what is meant by spiritual rebirth and salvation: the future resurrection of the body means that within the natural body (*Körper*) of the faithful, will be born

> a delicate, spiritual body [*Leib*], a hidden sideric or etheric, an independent, imperishable body. . . . Body remains body, spirit remains spirit: but the spirit comes from the body; the body however does not become spirit, it remains the vehicle of the spirit. Spirit cannot exist without a spiritual body, which is nourished from the life of Jesus, the Lord and Sovereign of life, who has life itself within him. *For bodiliness is the end of God's works* [*denn Leiblichkeit ist das Ende der Werke Gottes*].[120]

This last sentence, no doubt Oetinger's most famous saying, is usually quoted with reference to its appearance in his *Biblisches und emblematisches Wörterbuch*, art. "Leib."(Oetinger [1776] 1999, 222–223) It means—and this is crucial to any understanding of Oetinger's thought—that the body is not considered an imperfection that needs to be transcended, but a supreme divine gift that needs to be purified and transmuted in order for it to attain to its state of perfection.

Oetinger vehemently opposes his incarnational theosophy to what he considers the "satanic" doctrine of docetism. Docetism is the very essence of the antichrist, can be traced to the gnostic Cerinthus (fl. ca. 100 A.D.), and is continued in his own time by the perspectives of Leibniz and Wolff:[121]

> What is idealism? A panic-reaction[122] to materialism. Ach! who could make understandable, from the history of the devil, how he has maneuvered from century to century to pour this fright, this human fear, this worldliness, into the hearts of most of the philosophers and theologians, so that God's words, which should

bring forth in us only massive and figurative concepts, are no longer explained according to their actual meaning, nor even according to juridical rules of interpretation, but according to the idealist and sadducean *Geisterey* and *Antigeisterey*, and according to predetermined opinions, by which one changes the rich concepts of *Scripture* into empty and enfeebled statements.

I will not give a definition of idealism before having said this one thing: according to idealism, Christ has not come in *Water*, *Blood* and *Spirit*, but only in Spirit; Christ's body is no more than an illusion, a mere phenomenon, [for] inside he is a purely spiritual being. Thus said Cerinthus, as can be read in Irenaeus. The entire *Letter of John* and the *Gospel of John* is written against this doctrine of Cerinthus. (Oetinger [1763] 1977, I, 136)

The philosopher is much too spiritual to allow the highest Intelligence to tell him that God sits on a throne, white and red, Jaspis and Sardis, and with the colors of the rainbow; but they [the philosophers] will see to their dismay that the Infinite gives himself a form and modality through the seven spirits. This is entirely contrary to the Leibnizian and Mohammedan philosophy. But he who does not philosophize cannot accept this philosophy, for it is Cerinthian, it leads to the result that Christ has not come in the flesh. Hermes says: he who fears God, philosophizes up to the ultimate (Oetinger [1776] 1999, 253–254 [lemma "Philosophia"]).[123]

It was only gradually that Oetinger began to realize that Swedenborg might actually be a representative of the very "cerinthian" perspective considered by him to be the essence of the antichrist. As pointed out by Ernst Benz, Oetinger clearly began to distance himself after November 8, 1768, when Swedenborg sent him a small tract 'that he had written, titled "About the Natural and the Spiritual Meaning of the Word." In this work, Swedenborg describes what happens to theologians after their death: in heaven they are instructed about the fact that Swedenborg's method of exegesis is the only true one, and their subsequent salvation or damnation depends upon whether they accept or reject that fact. Swedenborg was thinking here mostly of the deists and rationalists, but Oetinger understood it as directed at him personally: ". . . Swedenborg threatens me, that when I do not accept his doctrine, I will be sent *ad inferiora* after my death."[124]

In the following year, Oetinger became more and more explicit in his criticism of Swedenborg's method of exegesis,[125] and from several writings published from 1770 to 1772, it becomes clear that he has begun to perceive in Swedenborg a representative of the "cerinthian" idealist school. He had been reading the writings of the rationalist-idealist theologian Johann Salomo Semler (1725–1791), who argued that the book of Revelation was inauthentic and should be removed from the canon; and he was struck by the similarity with Swedenborg's perspective. Both Semler and Swedenborg, he concluded, rejected the hard literal sense of Scripture and tried to eliminate from it whatever they happened to find offensive; Semler's rationalist approach turned out to be the logical end result of the idealist and allegorical method of exegesis practiced by Swedenborg, which got rid of any problem posed by the concrete contents of the Bible by changing them into abstract concepts. When Oetinger discussed the book of Revelation in his *Biblisches und emblematisches Wörterbuch* of 1771, his object of criticism was undoubtedly Swedenborg quite as much as Semler; but at the same time the passage below illustrates with particular clarity why Oetinger had so long remained ambivalent about Swedenborg:

> It is a very gross opinion, to take recourse to the pretext that the things of Revelation can be set aside, because what is mainly important for reaching salvation is in the words of Jesus and the Epistles of the apostles. And even when they read the holy Revelation, which is easier to understand than much in the Epistles (2 Peter 3, 16), they interpret it as if what is in fact actual and corporeal were written in a veiled manner; they think that in the invisible world all is spiritual, while actually hearing, tasting, feeling, smelling, eating, drinking takes place there in a much more real manner [*eigentlicher*] than in this lower world. They do not know what spiritual means. Spiritual is also bodily, but immaculate, imperishable, never withering away (1 Peter 1, 4), about which one will be happy with an unspeakable beatified joy (2 Thess. 1, 10). Heaven or the invisible world contains whatever may satisfy the eyes with the loveliest colors and beauties, the ears with musical instruments and songs, the nose with the most

> penetrating of smells, the palate with the sweetest food and drink,
> and the feelings with the things of the Song of Songs.[126]

Although Swedenborg is not explicitly mentioned here, the passage discusses the main two strands of his work—scriptural exegesis and visionary
experiences of the invisible world—in close connection. Oetinger once more
rejects the allegorical approach to scriptural exegesis in favor of a concrete
and literal understanding; and in doing so, he describes the things of the
invisible world as supremely "real" even in comparison with what we consider real in our world. Swedenborg had described heaven in precisely the
same way. His visions must have been irresistible to Oetinger because they
described the highly concrete "sensual" realities of heaven more clearly and
in greater detail than any author known to him. It is therefore psycholog-
ically understandable that he tried to turn a blind eye to any suspicions he
might have had that the very person who gave such wonderfully concrete
descriptions of heaven might turn out to be an adherent of the "cerinthian
perversion" when it came to the bodily presence of the divine in *this* world.

The proof of such bodily presence for Oetinger was the Bible itself,
taken in its literal sense; and the event *par excellence* in which God would
bodily manifest himself for all to see was, of course, the second coming of
Christ predicted in Revelation. Given the centrality of that event for
Oetinger, it became impossible for him to further ignore Swedenborg's
"cerinthianism" after he had received a copy of the latter's *Vera christiana
religio* in 1771. To begin with, Oetinger believed in Bengel's prediction that
Christ would return in 1836, and would therefore be highly skeptical of
any alternative dating. In 1768, however, Swedenborg had made a somewhat mysterious reference to an event that would take place as soon as
1770: "In two years one will see the doctrine of the New Church, predicted by the Lord in Revelation 21–22, appear in its fullness—in pleni-
tudine."[128] Swedenborg had in fact been thinking here of a book of his that
would be published in that year (Benz 1947, 205), but Oetinger misunderstood it as a prophecy about the coming of the New Church itself and
had decided to use it as a touchstone for judging the truth of Swedenborg's revelations. The year 1770 came and went without a sign of the
New Church; but what did come was Swedenborg's book *True Christianity*, with mottos from Daniel 7 and Revelation 21 about the coming of the

Son of Man and the Heavenly Jerusalem. Here Oetinger now read, to his horror, that Swedenborg completely denied any actual return of Christ and interpreted the biblical prediction in a purely metaphorical sense. Christ would not make his appearance bodily and in person, but only in a spiritual sense, for the "second coming of Christ" actually meant nothing but the final revelation of the true internal sense of Scripture. The Bible speaks of Christ arriving in power and glory on the clouds of heaven; but those clouds mean "the literal sense" while the power and the glory mean "the internal sense."[129] This was already bad enough from Oetinger's perspective, but it got worse. Swedenborg made it very clear that the "second coming of Christ" meant the appearance not of a person but of a book: his own *True Christianity*. In other words, it was through Swedenborg himself that Christ had "returned to earth;"[130] and this had happened on a very precise day, which had been a cause of celebration in heaven itself:

> After this work [*True Christianity*] had been finished, the Lord gathered his twelve disciples who had followed him in the world, and the next day he sent all of them out into the entire spiritual world, to preach the Gospel. . . . This happened in the month of June, on the 19th day, in the year 1770. (*True Christianity* §791)

True Christianity contains vehement polemics against anybody who believes that Christ will bodily return to earth, and against these backgrounds, Oetinger could no longer deny the complete incompatibility between Swedenborg's perspective and his own. On August 17, 1771, he writes to a friend: "Swedenborg has sent me his new book, and in it his wiles are revealed at last. The future of Christ should not be taken according to the letter. He [Swedenborg] is supposed to be the future" (Oetinger to Hartmann, August 17, 1771, as quoted in Benz 1947, 215).

It must have been very painful for Oetinger to admit to himself that his enemies had been right all along. It was now his turn to warn others, as in a revealing letter to a Rector Hasencamp from Duisburg:

> Mr. Pastor Henke has . . . reported that you had spread Swedenborg's doctrines. Due to his recently published book, I am, however, very worried about him. I send you the book, from which

you will see how much he is against us. I ask you to bring out a book in defense of the literal sense [of the Bible] and write down in it my objections as well as your own, because he denies the most important doctrines of Scripture. For he denies the white horse, he denies the two witnesses, he denies the three angels, he denies Christ's office of high priest, he denies the veritable and true idea of salvation . . . , he denies the content of the letter to the Hebrews and is thus entirely in agreement with Semler, against whom I have published the book about the materialism of the Holy Scripture and in which I have also refuted the Leibnizians' abstractions and debodifications [*Entkörperungen*] of apocalyptic expressions. He denies the thousand-year reign, he denies the city of God, and I'm afraid that he will yet cause a complete destruction of [biblical] interpretation. I much regret that originally, because he confirmed the below and the above after death, I have given him support in my first writings: I did this only because I did not yet know that instead of the future of Christ he would be selling a mere symbol [*Sinnbild*]. For he says that Christ will not come in person but only in the word, to build the new heaven and the new earth; the [personal] future of Christ, however, is supposedly presented in his [Swedenborg's] person. All this is flatly against our doctrines. Therefore prepare yourself to defend the teachings of the Reformers before the Augsburg confession. . . . Mr. Osiander[131] agrees with me. He [Swedenborg] draws from the correspondences more conclusions than is permitted. . . . On the one hand we prophesize, on the other hand we have faith. This is how things stand with us. We are dust, so let us not speak too cleverly, even though we are full of confidence in the fullness of faith. (Oetinger to Hasencamp, October 17, 1771, as quoted in Benz 1947, 218–219)

One well understands Oetinger's confusion when the news reached him, in 1771, that Swedenborg himself was planning to visit Württemberg. How should he receive the man he had been defending for years (although with many qualifications, as we have seen) but in whom he had now come to recognize an opponent of all he believed in, a representative of the "cerinthian" system of the antichrist? He was spared the ordeal, however: Swedenborg died the year after and never made it to Württemberg.

Swedenborg in Oetinger's Last Works

Having already taken a look at Oetinger's discussions of Swedenborg in his *Lehrtafel* (1763) and *Swedenborgs und anderer Irrdische und himmlische Philosophie* (1765), in conclusion let us briefly examine how Swedenborg appears in the two other major books published by Oetinger in the last period of his life: *Die Metaphysic in Connexion mit der Chemie* (Metaphysics in connection with Chemistry; 1771) and the *Biblisches und emblematisches Wörterbuch* (Biblical and Emblematic Dictionary; 1776).

Due to the publication ban, *Die Metaphysic* was published under the name of Oetinger's son, Halophilo Irenäo Oetinger. Like the *Lehrtafel*, it is a highly unsystematic work, interspersed with complete treatises by authors other than Oetinger himself (Johann Joachim Becher, Georg Ernst Stahl, Hermann Boerhaave, Johann Ludwig Fricker, Claude-Nicolas Le Cat, Guillaume Postel), some of them in Latin. We have already seen how Oetinger in the *Metaphysic* discusses the doctrine of signatures as providing only provisory and fragmentary empirical knowledge because of the as-yet-imperfect state of nature. Having pointed out that the doctrine of signatures is basic to *theologia emblematica*,[132] Oetinger uses the occasion to warn against "heteroclite" scriptural exegetes like Swedenborg, "whom one must severely contradict in this respect, although his other things *de statu post mortem* are not as ridiculous as they might seem":

> Swedenborg thinks quite mistakenly that the symbolic reference to the invisible is the core and the essence of Holy Scripture. The literal understanding, for example of the white horse, the walls, gates, the height, length and breadth of the new Jerusalem are supposedly there only to fill up the images; this is supposed to be only the outer shell, inside of which the *sensus internus* lies like the core, and in the end the shell falls away. The exegetical method . . . knocks to the ground what is most important in Holy Scripture, and although Swedenborg has threatened that whoever does not follow him will be degraded over there [that is, in

heaven], one should not care about that, for if somebody adds or
detracts something from the certain and truthful, plain words,
God threatens him with a greater degradation. (H. I. Oetinger
1771, 25)

This is not to deny, as he points out on the next page, that "there are many
mystical enigmatic things in Holy Scripture, which must be understood
emblematically;" but clearly such emblematic interpretation respects the
"massive" sense of the letter and does not cause it to evaporate into empty
abstractions.

In a long treatise on musical and number symbolism based upon the
system of his friend and pupil Johann Ludwig Fricker (1729–1766) (cf.
Henck 2001), Oetinger admits that Swedenborg gives useful information
about the inhabitants of heaven; but he adds that his *sensorium* can grasp
only some dimensions of the spiritual world. Swedenborg should have mod-
estly accepted his limitations, instead of thinking he could grasp the whole
of spiritual reality (H. I. Oetinger 1771, 452–453, and cf. 457).

Further in the *Metaphysic*, we find an "Apology by a Politician and Friend
of Mr. Prelate Oetinger against the Göttinger Review about the Metaphysics of Ezechiel, Jac. Böhme and Newton." We may safely assume that
Oetinger himself wrote this response to the review in *Göttinger Anzeigen
von gelehrten Sachen* 26/27 (1766) which, as we have seen, had occasioned
the publication ban. Full of indignation, the author criticizes the unfair-
ness of the reviewer, who has the audacity to ridicule even "the great Newton;" and very significantly he attempts to minimize the role of Swedenborg in Oetinger's book of 1765: "Swedenborg is not the main subject of
the book, but is included as by accident. . . . Mr. Prelate has merely under-
taken a critical investigation of Swedenborg: the main subject is the psychology of Ezekiel" (H. I. Oetinger 1771, 474).

Apart from two passing references, this is what Oetinger has to say
about Swedenborg in the *Metaphysic*. Since the book was published in 1771,
it must have been finished before or around the time that *Vera christiana
religio* opened Oetinger's eyes. Already two years earlier, however, Oetinger's
problems with Swedenborg's doctrine of signatures had inspired him to the
idea of refuting it by a book on emblematic theology. In February 1769,
he wrote to Hartmann: "What I have put down about emblematic theol-

ogy is very crude. Is directed against Swedenborg, who misuses the signature. He makes the signature look ridiculous."[133] Probably he was referring to his work on the new and greatly expanded version of his *Biblisches und emblematisches Wörterbuch*, an embryonic version of which had already appeared as part of his *Reden nach dem allgemeinen Wahrheits-Gefühl* in 1759. However, when that expanded version appeared in 1776, it was officially directed not against Swedenborg but against a typical product of rationalist exegesis, Wilhelm Abraham Teller's (1734–1804) bestselling *Wörterbuch des neuen Testaments* (1772). In no other work of Oetinger do we find his doctrine of *Geistleiblichkeit* expressed with such passion and at such length.

Swedenborg's name does not loom large in the *Wörterbuch*: we may assume that, by the time it was reaching its completion, Oetinger had more or less gotten over the trauma. No longer do we find any attempt at a systematic refutation; Swedenborg is merely mentioned in a number of lemmas and never in a positive sense. In the lemma *"Christus"* Oetinger remarks that Swedenborg has violated the meaning of the Second Coming, and the same point is made in the lemma *"Erscheinung, Epiphania, Optasia."* Under *"Paradiss, Paradisos,"* he remarks that some important ideas about the subject are absent from Swedenborg as well as Böhme. In the lemma *"Phantasia,"* he suggests that Swedenborg's fantasy was led astray. In *"Stadt Gottes-neu Jerusalem,"* he writes that "Schwedenborg transforms the city of God into a play of thoughts and invents instead a community on earth, which however does not arrive." Finally, in his appendix about Revelation, he writes full of irritation about Swedenborg's "misinterpretations," concluding that "Swedenborg will have to answer for his mystical extravagances. What must be taken symbolically, one should take as such. It is easy to see what is symbolic. Things that are impossible merely according to philosophy should not right away be taken as veiled or symbolic."[134] And thus we see that the man who had been responsible more than anyone else for spreading Swedenborg's fame in the German context ends up rejecting him as a danger to the true faith.

❧ 8 ❧

Immanuel Kant

MUCH HAS BEEN WRITTEN ABOUT IMMANUEL KANT'S RELATION TO
Emanuel Swedenborg,[135] but much less would have been necessary if specialists on these two thinkers had been more willing to learn from each
other. Most specialists on Swedenborg have insufficient training in philosophy to be entirely convincing in discussing the issues at stake, whereas
the discussions by Kant specialists tend to be flawed by a serious lack of
familiarity with Swedenborg's thinking, combined with an attitude of gra-
tuitous arrogance towards it.[136] Only recently has this situation been
improved by the dissertation and publications of Gregory R. Johnson, based
upon critical analysis of the historical sources pertinent to both Kant and
Swedenborg and combined with an acute understanding of the relevant
philosophical debates. If the following discussions will in some respects
come to conclusions different from those reached by Johnson, they are nevertheless indebted to his work.[137]

The Knobloch Letter and the Herder Fragments

The earliest relevant document is a letter by Kant to a Charlotte von
Knobloch, dated August 10, 1763.[138] It shows that, in response to an
inquiry by this lady, Kant made some investigations to find out the truth
about the stories concerning Swedenborg's miraculous abilities. The letter
is important because of its differences with respect to Kant's notorious
Träume eines Geistersehers (Dreams of a Spirit-Seer) published three years
later. Kant spells Swedenborg's name correctly, whereas three years later
he miswrites it as "Schwedenberg;" he knows that Swedenborg is a well-
known scholar (*ein Gelehrter*) and speaks about him with respect as "a rea-

sonable, agreeable, and sincere man," whereas three years later he calls him "a certain Herr Schwedenberg, without office or employment" and characterizes him depreciatingly as some unknown fool, "the arch-spirit-seer among all spirit-seers" and "the arch-dreamer among all dreamers" (*Erzphantast unter allen Phantasten*).[139] Swedenborg has promised to send him his most recent book, and Kant writes that he is eagerly awaiting it, whereas three years later he gives the impression of knowing only *Secrets of Heaven*, which he did not receive as a gift but paid for dearly with his own money; and he seems favorably impressed with the evidence for Swedenborg's miraculous gifts, whereas three years later he dismisses the evidence as wholly misleading.

The differences are not too difficult to account for.[140] In 1763 Kant must have developed a certain curiosity about Swedenborg, but he did not yet have any reason to get upset about him. Miss Knobloch's request did not seem to touch on serious philosophical matters, let alone on Kant's own philosophy: it was merely a matter of finding out what to think about the stories of Swedenborg's alleged clairvoyant abilities, and then writing a polite letter that would satisfy the lady's curiosity. Particularly interesting, in view of later developments, is the diplomatic manner in which Kant takes the occasion to distinguish between knowledge and truth:

> . . . notwithstanding all the stories of apparitions and actions of the kingdom of spirits, of which a great many of the most probable are known to me, I have always considered it to be most in agreement with the rule of common sense to lean to the side of denial; not as if I presumed to have seen into its impossibility (for how little do we know of the nature of a spirit?), but rather because on the whole it is not sufficiently proved. . . . (Kant [1766] 1976b, 100)

As will be seen, these sentences foreshadow a point that is crucial for understanding Kant's intentions in *Träume*. It may be possible in theory that a spiritual world exists; but as long as we do not have proof, we have no particular reason to assume that it exists, and it is more reasonable to assume the opposite. As will be seen, in his *Träume* Kant still maintains that a spiritual world as described by Swedenborg might possibly exist; but he has now come to the conclusion that, as a matter of principle, such existence is impossible to either prove or disprove by any rational or empirical criteria. Any positive statement about a spiritual world is irrational, not because the notion of such a world is absurd in itself, but because it is impossible for us to know it, even if it in fact exists.

Shortly after the Knobloch letter, during the academic year 1763–1764, Kant was lecturing on metaphysics. From surviving student notes, known as the *Herder Metaphysics* and *Herder Supplements*, we learn that, in this context, he sometimes referred to Swedenborg and was now apparently familiar with *Secrets of Heaven*. As has been carefully pointed out by Gregory Johnson, these and other student notes of Kant's lectures have to be read with great caution;[141] but nevertheless they do allow us to draw some conclusions about the role of Swedenborg's ideas in Kant's development. Kant refers to Swedenborg in a partly condescending and partly respectful manner: he "may really be a dreamer (*Phantast*)"[142] but should not be scorned. Plato and Apollonius of Tyana have reported similar visions. The majority of ghost stories are probably not to be trusted, but one should not too easily dismiss them as false and call their defenders liars: it is more correct to reserve judgment and say that they are not proven (see Kant [1766] 1976b, 107–108).

Kant must have begun writing his *Träume eines Geistersehers*, or at least have begun talking about the project, sometime during 1764, for Johann Georg Hamann (1730–1788) refers to it in a letter to Moses Mendelssohn dated 6 November of that year.[143] Unusual for Kant, the book was sent to the publisher page by page rather than as a complete manuscript, and in "very illegible" form. As a result, the publisher sent it to the censor (a standard procedure at the time) not in manuscript form, as required, but as printed copy, which caused him to be fined the considerable sum of 10 Thalers (Kuehn 2001, 171). It was published anonymously, but Kant made no great efforts to hide his identity as the author.

Dreams of a Spirit Seer

From the Prelude to *Träume*, we learn that people kept bothering Kant with questions about Swedenborg,[144] so that he finally decided to buy *Secrets of Heaven* and make up his own mind once and for all.

Since it is just as much a foolish prejudice to believe without reason none of the many things which are recounted with a semblance of truth, as it is to believe without proof all that is spread by popular rumor, hence the author of this work, in order to avoid the former prejudice, has allowed himself, partly at least, to be carried away by the latter. He confesses, with a certain humiliation, to having been naïve enough to investigate the truth of some of the stories of the kind mentioned. He found—as usual where one has no business to be—he found nothing. Now doubtless this is in itself already sufficient cause for writing a book; but add to that . . . the vehement urging of known and unknown friends. Furthermore, a large work had been purchased, and, what is even worse, had been read, and such effort should not be wasted. From this originated the present treatise, which, as one flatters oneself, should leave the reader in a state of complete satisfaction, since he will not understand its most important part, will not believe the other, and will ridicule the rest. (Kant [1766] 1976b, 6)

So this is how Kant came to buy the "large work" elsewhere referred to as "eight quarto volumes full of nonsense" known under the title *Secrets of Heaven*. Most remarkable about the Prelude, and indeed about the *Träume* as a whole, is Kant's tone of mockery about a subject to which he had, after all, devoted a considerable amount of time and energy. He begins right away by evoking the boundless "shadowland [which] is the paradise of dreamers," with its "hypochondriacal vapors, wet nurse tales, and cloister miracles" (Kant [1766] 1976b, 5), as apparently the proper context for his treatise. This "gothic" opening scene[145] may seem quite ill-chosen for a treatise on a visionary as dry and rationalistic as Swedenborg; but it is illustrative of the associations that any reference to "spirits" was bound to evoke in the mind of Enlightenment ideologues (and in fact, evokes even today).

The first, "dogmatic" part of *Träume* does not actually mention Swedenborg at all. Chapter one deals with the general problem of how one could rationally conceive of a "spiritual world." Kant does not ask himself whether spirits actually exist, but how we would have to conceive of them *if* they existed. On the basis of a thought experiment, he concludes that they would have to be conceived of as immaterial beings (Kant [1766] 1976b, 10).[146] Such a concept may be incomprehensible to us, he says, but incomprehensibility does not mean impossibility. It is not irrational to accept the theoretical *possibility* of immaterial beings; but that such beings do actually *exist* is impossible to either prove or disprove. If they do happen to exist, he continues, they must be somehow present in the material world without interfering with it: they must be active in space without filling space. If we assume that the human soul is a spirit, we cannot assume it to be located in any particular part of the body (such as the head, or the heart): Kant says that it must be wholly present in our whole body and wholly in each of its parts.

But while discussing such hypothetical possibilities—as well as alternatives such as those that locate the human soul in a "microscopically small spot of the brain" (Kant [1766] 1976b, 15)—Kant makes clear that we are actually talking about things we do not really understand. There are too many unknown and probably unknowable variables, and quite possibly we are wasting our time discussing chimaeras. Rather than talking about theoretical possibilities only, we should ask ourselves what would be the implications of believing that they are true. Thus, the theorist may be shocked to discover that they may force us to assume, for example, the possibility of reincarnation (Kant [1766] 1976b, 17–18).[147]

Having come to this point, Kant admits to the reader that he has himself a weakness for such metaphysical dreams: "I confess that I am much inclined to affirm the existence of immaterial natures in the world and to place my own soul in the class of these beings" (and in a footnote he adds that the roots of this inclination are obscure to himself and will probably remain so). In other words, the "dreams of metaphysics" referred to in the title have been dreamed by Kant himself! And the philosopher continues by pointing out how natural such dreams are. It really seems to us that "a spiritual being is most inwardly present in the matter with which it is combined and acts . . . upon the inner principle of their state. For every substance, even a simple element of matter, must after all have some kind of inner activity as the ground of its external efficacy, although I cannot specify in what it consists" (Kant [1766] 1976b, 19). These are eminently Swedenborgian formulations. The reader begins to understand what is at stake for Kant: those who dream the dreams of metaphysics, even if they are respectable philosophers, might eventually find themselves in the disreputable company of spirit-seers such as Swedenborg.

In his second chapter Kant quickly returns to the tone of mocking irony with which he began his book, by evoking the vaguely amusing image of "the initiate" who—once having accustomed himself to moving from crude sensory understanding to the higher domain of abstract thought—just stands there peering into the gloomy twilight of metaphysical shadows, where he dimly perceives the shapes of spiritual beings. No doubt the "initiate" is Swedenborg, but the name is still not mentioned. Kant continues by opposing the realm of dead matter, ruled by mechanical/mathematical laws, and the organic realm of beings who have some inner principle of life. The existence of the latter easily leads to the belief in immaterial "pneumatic" beings as the active powers that must be at work in organic beings; and from there, one is no less easily led to the belief that all these beings together form an immaterial, intelligible world. This *mundus intelligibilis* is then seen as an autonomous, self-subsisting, integrated whole, whereas the material world has to be seen as dependent on it: ". . . then one conceives of a grand whole of the immaterial world: an immeasurable but unknown hierarchy of beings and active natures through which alone the dead stuff of the corporeal world is animated" (Kant [1766] 1976b, 22–23). Anyone who might still doubt that Kant is thinking here of Swedenborg's worldview specifically, will be finally convinced by the following quotation:

> The human soul, already in this present life, would have to be regarded as simultaneously tied to two worlds, of which it, insofar as it is united with a body into a personal unity, clearly experiences only the material one, while, as a member of the spirit world, it receives and imparts the pure influxes of immaterial natures, so that, as soon as that union has ceased, all that remains is the community with spiritual natures, in which it stands at all times, and which must open itself to its consciousness in crystal-clear vision. (Kant [1766] 1976b, 25–26)

The reader seriously begins to wonder whether Kant is still being ironic, when he continues by remarking that he is getting tired of speaking in the careful language of reason and states that such a worldview "is as good as demonstrated, or it could easily be proven . . . or better still, will be [proven] in the future." Having described a few more explicitly Swedenborgian aspects of it, he concludes that it would be splendid if it could be deduced not merely from the all-too-hypothetical concepts of spiritual nature as such, but from real and universally acknowledged *observation*.

This is followed by an excursus about the human "moral sense," which could be explained in terms of a spiritual worldview; the description of the latter is again specifically Swedenborgian, but still without mention of Swedenborg's name. Returning to the main line of his discussion, Kant concludes that, given the strength of the arguments adduced so far, "scarcely anything appears more strange than the fact that community with spirits is not a wholly common and ordinary thing" (Kant [1766] 1976b, 33). The extraordinary thing, rather, would seem to be the *scarcity* of spirit phenomena. This leads Kant to a discussion about the relation between spiritual ideas and theoretical representations, on the one hand, and concrete spiritual visions, on the other: it is reasonable to assume that the former appear to us clothed in, or mediated by, the symbolic language available to the person who has the visions. The spiritual influx cannot be experienced in unmediated form, but only by evoking related images in the imagination, and that is where the problem is: the original spiritual sensation inevitably gets mixed up with the chimaeras of the visionary's personal imagination, so that it is impossible to distinguish the genuine spiritual core from the crude illusions that surround it.

Spiritual apparitions of this kind happen only in persons whose "organs of the soul" are unusually sensitive; and this sensitivity must be seen as an illness that causes the visionary to see hallucinations:

> representations that are by their nature alien to, and incompatible with, those that belong to the bodily state of human beings, press themselves forward and drag ill-assorted images into external sensation, through which wild chimaeras and wondrous caricatures are hatched out, which pass before the deceived senses in a long parade, even though they may have a genuine spiritual influx as their basis. (Kant [1766] 1976b, 37)

Kant emphasizes once again that, in evaluating ghost stories, the undoubted presence of chimaeric illusions is no sufficient reason to exclude the presence of genuine spiritual influxes (Kant [1766] 1976b, 38). But as far as the visionary himself is concerned, visionary knowledge of the other world can be obtained by him only at the price of losing some of the power of judgment needed for the present one. Or in other words, in order to be a genuine visionary, one has to be a little mad.

This is, in fact, the main theme of the third chapter, where Kant goes on discussing the "dreamers of experience"[148] as different from the "dreamers of reason." We may assume that, with the latter, he means the philosophers who lose themselves in abstract metaphysical speculation, whereas the former are spirit-seers such as Swedenborg; and Kant's discussion indicates that the two are intimately related. Kant goes into some detail about the nature of optical and auditory hallucinations, with details that are interesting but need not detain us here. Most important is that his discussion focuses on the nature of madness and its "higher grade," derangement (or ecstasy),[149] which is characterized by the fact that "the confused person transposes mere objects of his imagination outside himself and takes them to be things that are actually present before him" (Kant [1766] 1976b, 45).[150]

The conclusion of the chapter is nothing short of amazing, for its contents as well as its style. Having looked at the phenomenon of spirit-seers from what we would now call a psychiatric perspective, Kant states, with a hint of malice, that the outcome in fact "makes the profound suspicions of the previous chapter wholly superfluous" (Kant [1766] 1976b, 47). For even if he tends to look favorably on those metaphysical speculations about a spiritual world, the reader will certainly prefer an approach that "allows greater comfort and dispatch in decision, and can promise more general approval" (Kant [1766] 1976b, 47). It seems more reasonable to concentrate on facts of experience (that is, that spirit-seers are evidently mad) than to lose oneself in the deceptive mists of a half-poetic and half-argumentative speculation. And what is more, by taking such spirit-seers too seriously, the philosopher himself may become a target of ridicule and thereby render the reputation of philosophy a bad service.

It is remarkable to see how openly Kant is showing his cards here. Apparently one may well defend certain opinions and reject others, not on the strength of rational arguments but in view of public "approval" and concern about one's "reputation." And Kant seems to forget entirely his earlier, unambiguous, and repeated statement that the dreams of spirit-seers

may very well have their origin in genuine spiritual influx. Instead, he resorts
to a strategy of ridicule culminating in downright vulgarity:

> . . . in no way do I blame the reader if, instead of regarding the
> spirit-seers as half-citizens of the other world, he simply dismisses
> them without further ado as candidates for the hospital and thus
> spares himself all further inquiry. . . . [A]nd if it was once found
> necessary at times to *burn* some of them it will now suffice sim-
> ply to *purge* them. Nor would it have been necessary, since this
> is how matters stand, to range so far afield and, with the help of
> metaphysics, seek out mysteries in the fevered brains of deluded
> enthusiasts. The sharp-sighted Hudibras could alone have solved
> the riddle for us, for according to his opinion: If a hypochondri-
> acal wind rages in the guts, what matters is the direction it takes;
> if downwards, the result is a f---; if upwards, an apparition or a
> sacred inspiration. (Kant [1766] 1976b, 48)[151]

Kant himself now says that his previous chapter was superfluous, and what
was described there as a potentially genuine spiritual influx is here dis-
missed without further ado as the foul-smelling product of a "hypochondriacal wind in the guts." Philosophically there yawns, of course, a huge
gap in the argumentation; but Kant not only seems to believe it can be
filled by mere rhetoric, he does not even bother to try and cover up its
existence. He counts on it that his readers will take his side anyway, arguments or no arguments.

   In his fourth chapter Kant draws some conclusions. Having repeated
that he has tried to approach the problem of spirit stories with as little prejudice as possible, he again appears to feel the need to defend himself against
those who might criticize him for taking such a subject seriously at all. His
defense is quite weak: it may be true that ghost stories are merely a "plaything" for the philosopher and that one should not blow up the importance of such small matters, but occasionally one may nevertheless do so,
and the care with which one treats them might serve as an example to be
emulated in treating more weighty matters. This leads him to a more interesting point: the philosopher seeks to weigh the arguments pro and con-
tra a spiritual world on the scale of reason, but in truth this instrument

(*die Verstandeswage*) is not entirely impartial. This is because the philosopher cannot help being influenced by his personal and all-too-human hopes
that a future existence might await him after death: Kant, too, has to admit
that all the stories about spirits and a spiritual world do carry some weight
for him on "the scale of hope," even though they are like thin air on the
scale of rational speculation (Kant [1766] 1976b, 50). He goes as far as
confessing that the very direction of his own argumentations, in previous
chapters, betrays his own bias: for in discussing the relation between body
and spirit, they focused only on how the spirit might *leave* this world and
enter another one, while ignoring no less important questions such as how
the spirit might have *entered* the world by means of sexual reproduction
and how it might be *present* in this world at all. Kant writes that, in fact,
he has absolutely no idea about how the spirit might do any of these things
and would probably have been wiser not to try and address such questions
at all. He gave in to the temptation out of human weakness. In other words,
Kant so much as admits here that, at the time when he bought and studied Swedenborg's *Secrets of Heaven*, he did so not for philosophical reasons
only, but also because some part of him would like to be convinced of a
life after death.

   Since *Secrets of Heaven* failed to convince him, Kant is now somewhat
embarrassed about his own weakness, but he is honest enough to make it
explicit and takes care to restate his position of "methodological agnosticism" concerning a spiritual world.[152] Having confessed his total ignorance about any questions concerning the relation between spirits and matter, he emphasizes that "because of that very same ignorance I am not so
bold as to totally deny any truth in the various ghost stories, but with the
familiar yet strange proviso that I call any individual one into question, but
give some credence to all of them taken together. The reader remains free
to judge. . ." (Kant [1766] 1976b, 52). In other words, even if every single
example of Swedenborg's "things heard and seen" is doubtful, it is still possible that his spiritual world exists. However, Kant's earlier discussions have
shown once and for all that, although one may *think* all sorts of things about
spiritual beings, one cannot *know* anything about them (Kant [1766] 1976b,
52). And this leads him to a passage of crucial importance in the history
of philosophy.[153] For it is here that we see him, as it were, close the book
of positive metaphysics that had preoccupied him in his writings so far
and open a new one that will eventually lead to his mature *Kritiken*:

This assertion [that is to say, that it has now been established once and for all that we can never know anything about spirits] sounds rather arrogant. For certainly there is no object of nature known to the senses, of which it could be said that it is ever exhaustively understood by means of observation or reason, whether it be a mere drop of water, a grain of sand, or something even more simple: so boundless is the variety of that which nature even in its smallest parts presents for analysis to an understanding as limited as that of mankind. But with the philosophical concept of spiritual beings the situation is completely different. It can be completed, but *negatively*, in that reason securely establishes the limits of our understanding, and convinces us that the various phenomena of *life* in nature and their laws are all that is granted to us to know, whereas the Principle of this life, that is to say spiritual nature, which one does not know but only suspects [to be there], can never be positively thought, because no data about it are to be found in the whole of our sensations, and one must make do with negations in order to think something so very different from anything sensuous; and [in that reason convinces us] that even the possibility of such negations rests neither upon experience nor upon inferences, but upon a fiction into which reason, divested of all her tools, takes refuge. On this foundation, the pneumatology of man may be called a doctrine of his [man's] necessary ignorance with respect to a kind of beings that he suspects to exist, and as such it is easily adequate to its task.

And now I lay aside this whole matter of spirits—an extensive part of metaphysics—as settled and completed. From now on it will no longer be a matter of my concern. (Kant [1766] 1976b, 52–53)

Far from being a mere "plaything" of little philosophical concern, Swedenborg's worldview as presented in *Secrets of Heaven* provided the occasion for Kant to bid farewell to his "dreams of metaphysics" (dreamt, no doubt, during the "dogmatic slumber" from which he famously claimed to have been wakened by David Hume ([1711–1776]); Kant [1783] 1976a, 6–7) and enter the path that would lead him to cause a "Copernican revolution" in philosophy.

Swedenborg himself makes his explicit appearance in Kant's text only after this crucial point has been reached. In chapter one of the second, "historical" part, he is introduced as "a certain Herr Schwedenberg, without office or employment," who has been occupied for over twenty years with nothing but the spirit world and is certainly "the arch-spirit-seer among all spirit-seers" and "the arch-dreamer among all dreamers" (Kant [1766] 1976b, 56). Again, throughout the chapter, one is struck by Kant's defensiveness. First he wants to make sure that his readers will not suspect him of credulity (*Leichtgläubigkeit*); then he affirms, quite implausibly, that the whole question of spirit stories is unimportant and he himself is wholly indifferent (*Gleichgültig*) to such matters; and once he has nevertheless recounted the nowadays well-known stories about Swedenborg's miraculous clairvoyant powers, he hastens to explain to the reader why he wastes his time with such a "despised business" (*verachtetes Geschäft*) as passing on "fairy tales." His defense is again quite weak: after all, the philosophy discussed in part one is likewise a "fairy tale from the fool's paradise of metaphysics" (Kant [1766] 1976b, 59),[154] and why would blind faith in the sophistries of reason be more respectable than incautious belief in deceptive stories? Defending himself against ridicule remains Kant's main preoccupation for the rest of the chapter; by pointing out that many reasonable men have likewise been interested in superstitious beliefs, Kant feels that he is in sufficiently good company to be "shielded against mockery" and not "to be considered foolish."

Kant begins his second chapter by explaining to the reader why he has chosen to begin his book with a part about pure metaphysical abstractions and reveal only in part two that all this actually referred to a concrete empirical case: Swedenborg's visions. All knowledge, he points out, can be grasped in two ways: *a priori* or *a posteriori*, that is to say, starting from general principles of reason or from concrete empirical experience. The problem is that, if one chooses either of these two approaches, one finds that its results remain confined within its own boundaries and cannot be connected with the other in any non-arbitrary fashion. The philosopher's rational arguments and his empirical experiences or accounts are like two parallel lines that run on into infinity without ever crossing; and this is a problem because one clearly needs them both in order to make sense of reality. Many philosophers have tricked their readers (and no doubt themselves) into believing that the problem could be solved, but actually they exerted gentle pressure on their demonstrations so as to make them end up exactly where they wanted them to; as a result, it seems that "the lines cross," but this is an illusion created by a lack of rigor in their argumentation.

Kant begs his reader not to suspect him of such things and seems to want to convince him or her that the similarity between the metaphysics of part one and Swedenborg's worldview he is about to describe is a mere coincidence:

> Moreover, I have the misfortune that the testimony on which I have stumbled, and that bears such an uncanny likeness to my philosophical brainchild, looks desperately deformed and foolish. . . . Therefore I flatly state that, as concerns such offensive comparisons, I have no sense of humor and declare briefly and to the point that one should either suspect in Swedenborg's writings more cleverness and truth than first appearances allow, or that it is only by accident that his system coincides with mine. . . . (Kant [1766] 1976b, 64–65)

Swedenborg's "flask in the lunar world is completely full," and his *Secrets of Heaven* does not contain even one drop of reason: it consists, in fact, of "eight quarto volumes full of nonsense" (Kant [1766] 1976b, 65). Kant states right away that the "fanatic exegeses" concerning Genesis and Exodus are none of his concern and refers the reader to Ernesti's review. He is interested only in the visionary accounts. After some further invectives, he moves on to a description of Swedenborg's visionary states, his concept of internal versus external sense, the nature of Swedenborg's communication with angels, the non-spatial nature of angelic communities, the dependence of material on spiritual beings, the way in which angelic realities appear to the visionary, the "universal human," and the illusionary nature of space.

Particularly significant in Kant's short but generally correct summaries is the amount of attention he gives to Swedenborg's ideas about space; one cannot but be reminded here of his later concept of time and space as pure *Anschauungsformen*, developed in the "transcendental esthetics" of the *Critic of Pure Reason*, and the basic point that any reality where time and space (and causality) would not apply would be unknowable to us.[155] But having discussed Swedenborg's ideas at some length, Kant declares himself "tired of copying the wild chimaeras of this worst of all enthusiasts" and hopes that he will not be held responsible for the "mooncalves" that these summaries might cause to be born in his readers' imagination (Kant [1766] 1976b, 74–75). Having reminded those readers that they at least have not wasted seven pounds sterling on Swedenborg's *Secrets of Heaven*, Kant closes the section with some expressions of "shame" about how he has let himself be fooled.

Has Kant then been wasting his time in studying and discussing "a thankless subject" (Kant [1766] 1976b, 75)? Not really, he answers, for in doing so he did have a goal in mind, and he believes to have attained it: he has demonstrated the nature of metaphysics as the science of the limits of human reason:

> . . . metaphysics is a science of the *limits of human reason*, and since a small country always has many borders, and since it is more important to know well and guard one's properties than to go out blindly on conquests, therefore this use of the aforementioned science is at once the least known and the most important, though it is only reached fairly late and after long experience. I may not have precisely determined these limits here, but I have at least indicated them sufficiently for the reader to find, in further reflection, that he can exempt himself from fruitless inquiries concerning a question that requires data from another world than the one in which he finds himself. I have therefore been wasting my time while saving it. I have deceived my reader while benefiting him, and although I did not offer him a new insight, I have nonetheless destroyed the illusion and the vain knowledge that inflates the understanding and fills up the narrow space of the place that could be filled up with the teachings of wisdom and useful instruction. (Kant [1766]1976b, 76–77)

And that brings Kant to the concluding chapter of his book. We must know the limits of our human understanding and realize that, although there are many things we do not know, many of them we do not need either. Many questions, such as how my soul manages to move my body or how it might be or become related to other spiritual beings, cannot be answered by us except by self-created fantasies. If we give explanations without sufficient proof, we are not acting reasonably and deserve to be ridiculed, *even* if later generations might prove us right; likewise, a visionary like Swedenborg might be on the right track, but we are nevertheless foolish if we just believe him at his word.[156] We must accept our limitations and concentrate on what is most useful for living a moral life in the present world. The *Träume* ends with a reference to the conclusion of Voltaire's *Candide*: rather than wasting our time in vain scholastic disputes about things we will never know, we had better "cultivate our garden."

Early Reviews

Johann Gottfried Herder (1744–1803), who had studied with Kant from 1762–1764, reviewed *Träume* as early as March 1766; it is a verbose but rather noncommittal piece, which does not teach us much more than that Herder endorsed Kant's way of treating "enthusiasts."[157] More serious for Kant was the reaction by the great Jewish philosopher Moses Mendelssohn (1729–1786), who was then at the height of his fame. Kant sent his *Träume* to Mendelssohn on February 7, 1766, and respectfully asked him for his opinion. Mendelssohn's answer is no longer extant, but he apparently found the tone of Kant's book inappropriate for a subject as serious as metaphysics. In a lengthy letter to Mendelssohn, dated April 8, Kant sought to defend his approach.[158] He admits he found it difficult to discuss a subject like spirit visions without exposing himself to ridicule and decided to disarm his critics by ridiculing himself first. Most important for us, Kant confesses to Mendelssohn that, in spite of the "absurdities" of Swedenborg's spirit stories, he has a weakness for them, and in spite of the "obscure concepts" of the underlying metaphysics, he has "a certain suspicion concerning their correctness."[159] At the same time, however, he had experienced ever stronger feelings of aversion, even hatred, faced as he was with the "inflated arrogance of entire volumes full of insights of this kind" and based upon wholly false methods and approaches.[160] In sum, there might be some truth in Swedenborg's writings, but if so, it is in spite of his methods rather than thanks to them.

Kant writes that he is looking forward to the "more thorough reflections" that Mendelssohn has apparently promised; but, in fact, the latter's review of the *Träume* remained very short and showed that Kant had not succeeded in dispelling his misgivings: the combination of jest and pensiveness characteristic of the *Träume* makes it hard to decide "whether Mr. Kant's intention is to ridicule metaphysics or to make spirit-visions credible," and his important insights and new ideas would "deserve a more serious exposition."[161] As for Swedenborg, Mendelssohn seems completely uninterested, even to the point of worsening Kant's misspelling by referring to him as *Schredenberg*.

Another review, published simultaneously by the Lockean empiricist Johann Georg Heinrich Feder (1740–1821) (later a leading opponent of Kant's critical philosophy), likewise emphasized the excessively unacademic tone, as a result of which the reader often does not know whether the anonymous author—Feder does not seem to know that it is Kant—is joking or serious. Most interesting is Feder's suggestion that the author might actually be more indebted to Swedenborg than he cares to admit: "But would he now be capable of criticizing him so shrewdly, if it had not been by him that he had built himself a little system in the first place,[162] that he could subsequently expand, change, break down, and build upon . . . ?"[163]

The Later Lectures on Metaphysics

Contrary to what is commonly believed, Kant's *Träume* was not his last word on Swedenborg, and he continued to take his worldview more seriously than one might have expected. As has been demonstrated most completely by Gregory Johnson, Kant continued referring to Swedenborg for more than two-and-a-half decades after *Träume* and, in fact, touches on his ideas in all the surviving student notes of lectures about the state of the soul after death. As pointed out earlier, these notes must be treated with caution,[164] but there is no denying that they force us to look at Kant's attitude towards Swedenborg with more nuance than is usual in Kant scholarship.

Sometimes we are dealing with only passing references, to which we need attach no great significance.[165] But it is a different matter with the so-called "Metaphysik L 1" (1778–1779 or 1779–1780, that is to say, given during Kant's so-called "silent decade"). Here we find an extensive passage about the possible state of the soul after death, in which Swedenborg plays a remarkably positive role. Kant begins by rejecting the idea of survival of the spirit in bodily form (either by reincarnation or by means of a trans-figured body) and then proceeds to describe the option of survival as "pure spirit" in specifically Swedenborgian terms, with continuous emphasis on the non-spatial nature of heaven and hell. Reading these passages, one cannot but conclude that any acceptance of survival as pure spirit for Kant would be tantamount to accepting Swedenborg's worldview: he does not make any distinction between the metaphysical doctrine as such and Swedenborg as a specific version of it but treats the two as synonymous. Indeed, he concludes by saying that, although this opinion of the other world cannot be demonstrated, it should be seen as "a necessary hypothesis of reason, which can be opposed to opponents."[166] It is only at that point that he mentions Swedenborg, as the one whose thought on this matter is "very sublime [*sehr erhaben*]." The rest of the discussion is in line with the conclusions of *Träume:* the existence of spirits is possible although not provable; spirits cannot appear in the visible world through visible effects, and therefore Swedenborg could not have seen them either;[167] common sense tells us not to accept ghost stories; providence has "closed off the future world to us;" and the chief matter is always morality. We conclude that for Kant, at this time, Swedenborg stood for the doctrine of pure spirit *as such* and that he respected it as a possible, albeit unprovable, metaphysical position.

Essentially the same argumentation, but more condensed and without explicit mention of Swedenborg, is found in the "Metaphysik Mrongovius" (1781–1782). Having again described what is, in fact, the Swedenborgian concept of heavenly societies, Kant calls it "a marvelous representation" (*eine herrliche Vorstellung*).[168] Again, the same material is treated, with very much the same conclusions, in the "Metaphysik Volckmann" (1784–1785), which does mention Swedenborg.[169] Kant once more emphasizes the difference between truth and knowledge: "even if real ghosts exist, a rational person must still not believe in them." In the so-called "Metaphysik L 2" (1790–1791), the "Metaphysik K 2" (1791–1792 or 1792–1793) and the "Metaphysik Dohna" (1792–1793) we find mere variations on the same themes; Swedenborg is mentioned neither positively nor negatively, but merely as an author who has held certain positions discussed by Kant.

The exception that—as we will see—confirms the rule is the so-called "Fragment einer späteren Rationaltheologie nach Baumbach" (1789–1790

or 1790–1791). Kant here refers to Swedenborg's discussions of the inhabitants of other planets, a topic not touched upon in the *Träume*. Noting
that Swedenborg only spoke of the planets then known by astronomers,
but not about Uranus (discovered by William Herschel on March 13, 1781),
he dismisses Swedenborg without further ado as "a deliberate fraud."[170]
But other than might seem to be the case at first sight, this does not at all
contradict the respectful mention of Swedenborg and his worldview in
"Metaphysik L 1" and the other lectures mentioned above. Gregory Johnson argues that Kant displays a positive regard for Swedenborg in all his
lectures after *Träume* and is therefore forced to question the reliability of
this particular fragment.[171] But another explanation seems much more
likely. After *Träume*, Kant thought quite negatively about Swedenborg and
his visionary pretensions. The essential thing to notice is that the positive
references in the notes of his lectures are all about the nature of Swedenborg's metaphysical worldview *considered in and for itself*: Kant finds it "most
sublime" and "marvelous," but that means neither that it is also true (for
that is something we simply do not know), nor that Swedenborg's visions
can be accepted as evidence in favor of it (quite the contrary, as we have
seen), let alone that it implies any positive opinion about Swedenborg as
a person or as a visionary. Seen from this perspective, the apparent contradiction between the Baumbach fragment and the other lecture notes vanishes as snow before the sun: all Kant's later statements are not only compatible with, but follow naturally from, the distinction between knowledge
and truth that is basic to the *Träume*.

What Was at Stake?

This brings us to some conclusions about the celebrated case of Kant versus Swedenborg. The essential thing to notice is that Kant's concern is with
method, whereas Swedenborg's concern is with *truth*; or in other words,
Kant wants to establish how human beings can attain reliable knowledge,
whereas Swedenborg presents his knowledge to the reader. These are completely different concerns: one is epistemological, the other ontological.
Remarkably enough, Swedenborg appears to have been in complete agreement with Kant's basic epistemology: it is impossible for human beings to
discover the truth about heaven by themselves, for our common human

faculties are simply inadequate.[172] But whereas Kant concludes that therefore we cannot attain any knowledge of heaven, Swedenborg claims that
the abyss has been bridged "from the other side," that is to say, by the Lord
himself. Kant and Swedenborg agree that humanity cannot *discover* the
truth; but unlike Kant, Swedenborg claims that it can be *revealed* to human
beings. He knows this because it has happened to himself.

We begin to see how close the two opponents really are. For while Swedenborg would have accepted Kant's epistemological strictures, Kant for
his part had no great problems with Swedenborg's ontology either. On the
contrary, he personally found himself attracted to Swedenborg's worldview as presented in *Secrets of Heaven*. It provided a sublime perspective on
life after death, a perspective moreover that might happen to be true (that
is to say, it is theoretically possible) and one in which he would like to
believe. Would we not all like to believe that death is not the end? But
having admitted that much, Kant's Enlightenment instincts take over and
overrule his all-too-human longings: our concern should be with what is
true, not with what we would like to be true. The rational foundations of
our cherished beliefs must be subjected to critical scrutiny, and if they fail
to be convincing, we have no choice but to discard them as pious illusions.
The inflated arrogance of those who set themselves up as God's elected
spokesmen must be countered by the sober but reliable voice of reason.

The scholar of religions Jan Snoek has pointed out, in a different context, how the psychological need for emphasizing "difference" is amplified,
the greater the similarity between two positions actually is (Snoek 1995);
and it seems indeed that the same dynamic was strongly present in Kant's
reaction to Swedenborg. He found himself confronted with an author
whose work displays a highly rationalistic "Enlightenment" frame of mind,
quite similar to his own, and in whose worldview he recognized something very familiar as well: the idealistic metaphysics associated with Leibniz and Wolff that had occupied him for so many years.[173] Kant declared
himself to be "in love with metaphysics" and must have been profoundly
shocked to realize that claims of positive, empirical knowledge about metaphysical realities cause those realities to leave the comfortable and
respectable realm of abstract thought and take very concrete shape as a doctrine about spirits and ghosts very much like Swedenborg's. For, as formulated by Henri Delacroix, "the only difference [with the metaphysics of

the Wolffian school] is that Swedenborg believes in a real, empirical communication between the sensible and the intelligible world, whereas ordinary metaphysics merely assumes the possibility of such an exchange" (Delacroix 1904, 566). In Swedenborg's case, the dream of reason had created what Kant could only see as monsters:[174] the specter of a "gothic" world of "hypochondriacal vapors, wet nurse tales, and cloister miracles," in short, the world of the occult. The specter had to be exorcized at all costs, precisely because it was so uncomfortably close to Kant's own concerns. This explains not only why he took the trouble to study and criticize Swedenborg at such length, but also why *Träume* is by far the most emotional of all his writings. In a way, Kant was fighting his own shadow.

To understand his strategy in doing so, Michel Foucault (1926–1984) provides us with useful clues.[175] Foucault has analyzed the "procedures of exclusion" that structure human discourse and render it either acceptable or not. A first procedure is the use of *prohibitions*: certain kinds of discourse are forbidden because they are seen as threatening the moral order. A second procedure opposes *reason against madness*: the discourse of the madman may be excluded as irrational, but it has also been suspected of containing "a reason more reasonable than the one of the reasonable people" (Foucault 1971, 13). And a third procedure, finally, opposes *what is true against what is false*. Now, we have seen that Kant is very much concerned with being accepted by the representatives of "respectable" Enlightenment discourse. He is afraid that, by taking Swedenborg seriously—by being seen as including him within the domain of acceptable discourse—he might find himself excluded. Foucault's first dimension, prohibition, plays no clear role in how Kant handles the situation, but the other two dimensions do. The problem is that Swedenborg's worldview might well be true; and in order to dismiss it as false, Kant would be required to make positive statements about a domain—the metaphysical—which is not accessible to human reason. Therefore he takes recourse to the third dimension mentioned by Foucault: Swedenborg's worldview might be true, but Swedenborg himself is mad. It is only on *this* basis that he can be successfully excluded from acceptable discourse, while Kant himself remains included as representing the voice of reason against the ramblings of insanity.

Kant's strategy of exclusion proved successful. Historians of philosophy henceforth assumed they could understand *Träume* without needing to try and understand its subject of discussion. That such an approach is rational is doubtful at the very least, but that it served the interests of the Enlightenment project is certain.

9

Some Later Readers of *Secrets of Heaven*

ONE WONDERS HOW MANY AUTHORS IN GERMANY TOOK THE TROUBLE TO actually order Swedenborg's *Secrets of Heaven* and study it. Very often, we find that they refer not to the Latin original but to Oetinger's translations in his book of 1765; and not infrequently it is impossible to find out whether an author had read Swedenborg himself or only Oetinger's selections. About the following authors a bit more can be said.

Johann Georg Hamann, the great counter-Enlightenment philosopher often referred to as the "Magus of the North" (see Berlin 1993) was among those who did attempt to read *Secrets of Heaven*. In a letter written in 1784, he writes:

> The translation of Swedenborg does not allow one to understand the peculiarity of his Latin style, which really has something spooky. Just like our Kant, at the time, immersed himself in all the works of his [Swedenborg's] enthusiasm [*Schwärmerei*], I too have forced myself to go through the whole collection of heavy quarto volumes, which contains such a disgusting tautology of concepts and things that I found hardly enough in it to fill one leaf of paper. Abroad, I found an older work of his, *De infinito*, written entirely in the Wolffian-scholastic manner. For myself, I explain the whole miracle out of some kind of transcendental epileptics, dissolving in critical foam.[176]

Although Hamann does not say when it was that he read *Secrets of Heaven*, we may reasonably assume that he did so around the same time as Kant. Given the latter's opinion, it is hardly likely that he would have spent money on a copy of his own; much more probably, he had borrowed it from Kant himself.

The important Christian theosopher and physiognomist Johann Caspar Lavater seems to have become curious about Swedenborg as a result of reading Kant's book. His earliest references are found in his *Aussichten in die Ewigkeit* (Perspectives on Eternity; 4 volumes, 1768–1778). In the second volume, published in 1769, he writes about the transfigured body after death, and remarks:

> I wish that Kant of Königsberg had written something about that. But I'm afraid that a man who, although endowed with such rare philosophical genius, yet reasons so unphilosophically about the influence of a further reflection on the doctrine of the immortality of the soul and the nature of our future state in moral life, will not concern himself with such matters. It may be that his aversion against philosophizing about the future results from moral observations; perhaps he has seen many people who, the more they philosophized about the future, the more unworthy they lived; and that may be the reason why he prefers with Voltaire's *Candide* to go into the garden and plant fruits.[177]

Several scholars have argued that Lavater's famous physiognomy, as developed already in his *Aussichten* and culminating in his great *Physiognomische Fragmente* of 1775, is heavily influenced by Swedenborg (Benz 1938; Bergmann 1988). This might be the case, but unfortunately the precise connection cannot be established with certainty. It is true that *Secrets of Heaven* contains quite a lot of discussions relevant to physiognomy;[178] but, unfortunately, Ernst Benz, in what remains the most important study of the subject, contents himself with providing long parallel discussions of Swedenborg's and Lavater's physiognomical ideas, without ever addressing the question of which passages in Swedenborg Lavater might actually have read. The crucial point here is that Swedenborg's physiognomical discussions are *not* included in Oetinger's German translation;[179] therefore, they could only have influenced Lavater if the latter had actually read the complete Latin original. Whether he did can only be established by a detailed study that critically compares all Swedenborg's physiognomical passages in *Secrets of Heaven* with Lavater's ideas in his *Physiognomische Fragmente*; such a study should investigate whether the connections are sufficiently specific and should take into account other physiognomical works and traditions on which either Swedenborg or Lavater might have been dependent. Only on that basis would it be possible to establish, indirectly, that Lavater read *Secrets of Heaven*.

Much has been written about Swedenborg's influence on Johann Wolfgang von Goethe (see especially Morris 1899; Zimmermann 1969; Heinrichs 1979, 174–205; Gaier 1984 and 1988); but, as before, we will have to restrict ourselves to the influence of *Secrets of Heaven* specifically. In 1899 there appeared a much-quoted article by Max Morris, in which he argued that the first parts of Goethe's *Faust* I and the final parts of *Faust* II are filled with direct allusions to specific passages in *Secrets of Heaven*. Morris gave numerous quotations from the Latin original but neglected to answer one crucial question: do these references prove that Goethe actually used *Secrets of Heaven*? In 1984, Ulrich Gaier was able to answer this question in the negative: without any exception, all the passages quoted by Morris can also be found in Oetinger's translations in his book of 1765 and in his 1771 translation of Swedenborg's *De Telluribus* (which, as we have seen, is an only slightly re-edited version of the final parts of *Secrets of Heaven*'s "third strand," starting with §6695).[180] There is no evidence that Goethe ever read Swedenborg's Latin original, but we do know that Oetinger's first Swedenborg book stood in his father's library and that he himself bought a copy in 1776.[181]

In all likelihood, Goethe was introduced to Swedenborg by way of Fräulein von Klettenberg and her circle in Frankfurt, during the late 1760s, and his interest peaked during the years 1772–1773. This coincides with the period when he wrote his first version of *Faust* I. In 1773, he wrote a review of Lavater's *Aussichten in die Ewigkeit*, which contains the following sentences:

> Now may his [Lavater's] soul rise up . . . , and feel deeper into the spirit-whole [*das Geisterall*]. . . . To that end we wish him close community with the valued seer of our times, around whom was the joy of heaven, to whom the spirits spoke through all the senses and limbs, and in whose breast lived the angels: may his

glory shine around him, glow through him, that one day he may feel the heavenly bliss, and have an inkling of what is the babbling of the prophets, when *arreta rhemata* [unspeakable words] fill the spirit. (Goethe in *Frankfurter gelehrte Anzeigen* 37 (1773), 261)

Undoubtedly the "seer" is Swedenborg, and it is evident that, in these years, Goethe was enthusiastic about the spiritual worldview he had encountered in Oetinger's translations.

An analysis of Swedenborgian elements in Goethe's *Faust* and in his other writings would go far beyond the limitations we have set ourselves; but one detail must be addressed here. Turning away from the vain pursuit of science and learning, on which he has been wasting all his energies, Faust at the beginning of the drama turns to magic:

Flieh! auf! hinaus ins weite Land	Fly upwards! Out into the open space!
Und dies geheimnisvolle Buch	And this mysterious book
Von Nostradamus' eigner Hand	Written by Nostradamus's own hand
Ist dir es nicht Geleit genug?	Will it not suffice as your guide?
Erkennest dann der Sterne Lauf,	So understand the course of the stars,
Und wenn Natur dich unterweist	and when Nature teaches you,
Dann geht die Seelenkraft dir auf,	then the soul's power will arise in you,
Wie spricht ein Geist zum andern Geist	how one spirit speaks to another spirit.
Umsonst, dass trocknes Sinnen hier	In vain, that dry reflection here
Die heil'gen Zeichen dir erklärt	explains the sacred signs for you:
Ihr schwebt, ihr Geister, neben mir;	you, spirits, are floating next to me;
Antwortet mir, wenn ihr mich hört!	Answer me, if you hear me!

The references to invisible spirits might plausibly be interpreted along Swedenborgian lines, but of particular interest for us is the "mysterious book." Morris argued that the reference to Nostradamus (1503–1566) should not be taken too seriously: Goethe could not mention Swedenborg as its author, for the simple reason that the Faust story is situated in the sixteenth century. But in fact, or so he argues, the term *geheimnisvoll* (literally, full of secrets) demonstrates that he was in fact thinking of *Secrets of Heaven* (Morris 1899, 498). This suggestion has been adopted after Morris by quite a few later authors (see, for example, [Sewall] 1906, 19; Lütgert 1923, 210; Kirven 1988, 106). However, the term *geheimnisvoll* is far too common to be used as proof, and all the more so since there is no reference to the "heavenly" nature of the secrets. Furthermore, *Secrets of Heaven* was not a single book but consisted of no less than eight volumes. And finally, Faust explicitly devotes himself not just to commerce with spirits, but to *magic*. If, indeed, Goethe was thinking of a specific book not written by Nostradamus, a far more likely candidate would be Cornelius Agrippa's (1486–1535) famous compendium of magic, *De occulta philosophia* (1533).[182] Nothing can be proved here with certainty (it remains possible that Goethe was really thinking of Nostradamus, even though the latter wrote prophecies and was not concerned with magic or spirits); but given the lack of evidence in favor of Morris's thesis, it can safely be discarded as a myth.

We have scattered references to *Secrets of Heaven* having been studied by later authors. Thus, the writer August Strindberg read the first four volumes of the Swedish edition in the winter and spring of 1896–1897, together with a series of other works by Swedenborg. The descriptions of the hells frightened him, as is clear from a letter of December 17, 1896: "Am now reading Swedenborg's *Secrets of Heaven* and am terrified. It all appears to be true to me, and still, too cruel from a God of love. So I prefer *Séraphita*."[183] The reference is, of course, to Honoré de Balzac's influential novel about a Swedenborgian androgynous angel-spirit Seraphitus/Seraphita. The author on hermeticism and alchemy Ethan Allen Hitchcock (1798–1870) frequently quotes *Secrets of Heaven* in an (unconvincing) attempt at presenting Swedenborg as a "hermetic philosopher."[184] Helen Keller does the same, although for different purposes, in her *Light in my Darkness*;[185] the psychologist of religion William James (1842–1910) seems to have studied and annotated *Secrets of Heaven*,[186] and so on and so forth.

Undoubtedly the list could be considerably expanded, but again, it is usually hard or impossible to distinguish between an interest in Swedenborg's writings generally and in *Secrets of Heaven* specifically. Most readers appear to have focused on the "accounts of memorable occurrences" that can be found in other and later works as well. And the situation is further complicated by the phenomenon of indirect transmission of Swedenborgian concepts by way of authors such as, for example, Balzac.[187]

❦ EPILOGUE ❧

THE HISTORY OF SWEDENBORG'S *Secrets of Heaven* AND ITS RECEPTION IS not devoid of a tragic dimension. While Swedenborg spent countless hours on his extraordinarily detailed exegesis of (almost) each and every verse of Genesis and Exodus, very few readers outside the New Church ever seem to have been interested in this aspect of his work. Even such a biblicist theologian as Oetinger—not to mention Kant—appears at first to have quickly passed over the exegetical parts, to focus almost all his attention on the "accounts of memorable occurrences" (thus overlooking the abyss between Swedenborg's allegorical approach and his own literalism); and this attitude has remained dominant ever since. Swedenborg's lasting fame and influence are undoubtedly based upon his spectacular visions, not upon his tireless efforts as an interpreter of the Bible.

What remains is the unquestionable importance of *Secrets of Heaven* as a huge reservoir of religious ideas and concepts, from which emerged a comprehensive worldview of startling originality and internal consistency. It is not difficult to understand that Swedenborg's extraordinarily graphic and detailed visionary descriptions of heaven and hell were bound to appeal to the imagination of many readers; but it would be a mistake to see this "Romantic" appeal as the only reason for his wide-ranging influence up to the present day. A major key to understanding that influence lies in Swedenborg's *rationality*. His scientifically trained mind, used to the dry discipline of logic and always alert to the rational consistency of concepts, is dominantly visible throughout *Secrets of Heaven*; and many of the religious and moral questions that he sought to answer are those of a man of the Enlightenment. The result was a worldview based upon supra-rational revelation but presented in rationalist language and congenial to modern mentalities. It is, therefore, not surprising that basic Swedenborgian concepts came to be adopted by spiritualists and other occultists (whose "rationalism" is more pronounced than is often appreciated) during the nineteenth century and that they can be encountered even in contemporary "New Age" contexts that have no room for biblical exegesis.[188] Although Swedenborg himself would have seen such hybrid spiritualities as unfortunate mixtures of truth and falsity, from an historical perspective, they testify to the continued vitality of Swedenborg's thought.

❧ NOTES ❧

Introduction, pages xvii–xxiii

1. Traditional historiography was based upon the idea of a sharp and irreconcilable opposition in eighteenth-century culture and society between "Enlightenment and Reaction"; and such a perspective is still very influential today (see for instance Jonathan Israel 2001; 2006). It has been increasingly criticized, however, by German historians, in particular, who demonstrate that the relation between "religion and reason" was much more complex than previously thought and who call attention to the emergence during the eighteenth century of eclectic mixtures that sought to establish an alternative religious worldview compatible with science and rationality. Of pioneering importance in this regard was Rolf Christian Zimmermann's concept of a *"Vernünftige Hermetik"* (Enlightened Hermeticism) in eighteenth-century culture, presented in the first volume of his now-classic study of the worldview of the young Goethe (Zimmermann 1969–1979, I, 19–43). Recently, historians of the eighteenth century have developed similar perspectives; but whereas some of them retain the term "hermeticism" in this context (see, for example, Trepp and Lehmann 2001), others prefer to speak of "esotericism" rather than "hermeticism" (see, for example, Neugebauer-Wölk 1999a; 1999b; 2000; 2003).

2. For a critical overview of how Swedenborg has been perceived by academic Kant scholarship, see Hanegraaff forthcoming.

3. Since "the Lord" (*Dominus*) is the standard way of referring to God in Swedenborg's system, I will adopt this convention here.

4. That is to say, in his or her role of historian. Privately, of course, the historian may or may not believe in the existence of heaven; the point is that such personal beliefs cannot be verified or falsified by those who do not already share them. For a detailed discussion of "empirico-historical" research and the necessity in that context of "methodological agnosticism," see Hanegraaff 1995.

5. Jonsson 1979, 251. Here and in the rest of this book, translations from other languages are by the author, unless stated otherwise. Quotations from *Secrets of Heaven* are those of Lisa Hyatt Cooper in the NEW CENTURY EDITION OF THE WORKS OF EMANUEL SWEDENBORG (passages

from volumes later than the first one are based on the draft versions that were available at the time this book went to print).

6. On Western esotericism, see the foundational studies of Antoine Faivre (Faivre 1994; Faivre 2000a). See also Hanegraaff 1996–1998; Hanegraaff 2004c.

7. It is well known in Swedenborg scholarship that, in two separate letters to his friend Gabriel Beyer (1720–1779), Swedenborg denied ever having read Böhme (Tafel 1877, 251, 260) and, in the second letter, described his deliberate avoidance of the work of other theologians.

8. With respect to Swedenborg's alleged debt to the Jewish and Christian Kabbalah, see Hanegraaff 2004a. See also Roling 2006 for an interesting recent discussion that comes to partly different conclusions.

9. A possible line of influence that should be further investigated, not least in light of Swedenborg's lengthy sojourns in London, is the English Behmenist tradition, including authors such as John Pordage (1607 or 1608–1681) and Jane Leade (1623–1704). In reading the descriptions of visionary experiences by these and other Christian theosophers (for a useful selection, see Versluis 2000; and see also Versluis 1999), one cannot but be vividly reminded of Swedenborg's visions. But while quite some attention has been given to alleged Kabbalistic influences, references to the English Behmenists are strangely absent in the secondary literature. In exploring the possibility of such influences, however, one should not lose sight of the great differences between Behmenist theosophy and Swedenborg: for example, the former is based entirely on a specific doctrine of the Fall (or rather, several successive Falls) that has no parallel in the latter.

10. On Swedenborg's relation to this current, see Hanegraaff 2005, 1130–1131.

11. Whether Swedenborg's worldview should be categorized as "Western esoteric" depends on how one defines the latter domain. For an analysis with reference to Faivre's authoritative definition, see Williams-Hogan 1998, who concludes that one of Faivre's four "intrinsic characteristics" of Western esotericism—"living nature"—does not figure in Swedenborg. With respect to Swedenborg's influence on later esoteric traditions—as distinct from the development of the organized Swedenborgian New Church—see, for example, Brock et al 1988, Larsen et al 1988, Wilkinson 1996. It is clear that Swedenborgian ideas very quickly became syncretized

with various ideas of different provenance, many of which were actually at variance with Swedenborg's own views.

12. On the notion of "discourse" in the study of Western esotericism and the relation to notions of "tradition," see von Stuckrad 2005, 1–11. For a criticism of the idea of Western esotericism as a "counter-culture," "undercurrent," or "hidden tradition," and a concomitant emphasis on historical complexity, see Hanegraaff 2001.

13. For Oetinger as situated within the context of Western esotericism, see Breymayer 2005; for his role in Christian theosophy, see Faivre 2000a; for his importance to Christian Kabbalah, see Benz 1958.

14. Here I am thinking of Kant [1755] 1995 and [1764] 1960.

Chapter 1: A Key to the Secrets, pp. 3–11

15. Swedenborg's unpublished manuscript *Clavis Hieroglyphica Arcanorum Naturalium et Spiritualium, per Viam Representationum et Correspondentiarum* was translated into English by Robert Hindmarsh (1759–1835) in 1792 (=Swedenborg 1792); by James John Garth Wilkinson (1812–1899) in 1847 (=Swedenborg 1847); and by Alfred Acton (1867–1956) in the Swedenborgian journal *The New Philosophy* 1916–1917 (=Swedenborg 1916–1917; reprinted in Swedenborg 1984, 157–194). The quotations in the text refer to Acton's translation, which is the only one with added section numbers. Swedenborg's use of the term *hieroglyphics* obviously reflects an understanding of that term that predates the correct understanding of Egyptian hieroglyphs as it emerged in the wake of Champollion's deciphering of the Rosetta Stone; since the Renaissance at least, there existed a widespread discourse about hieroglyphs as a mysterious language possibly reflecting the original language of humankind (see, for example, Dieckmann 1970).

16. See Jonsson 1970, 308–309, about Swedenborg's dream of a *universal mathesis* (see also *Hieroglyphic Key* §25; as is common in Swedenborgian studies, text citations refer not to page numbers but to section numbers—in this case, those added by Acton in his translation of 1916–1917).

17. See, for example, *Hieroglyphic Key* §28 about the doctrine of the two suns: "In man or the microcosm there is no other sun than his soul or spiritual mind whence comes intelligence. But God is the sun of wisdom,

or wisdom itself, just as the sun of the world is the sun of light." See also §§30–31 about heaven and hell as states of being created by an individual's "loves": "Love of the highest good brings forth happiness, and this, heaven. . . . But love of evil brings forth unhappiness, and this, hell. . . . Heaven signifies the most perfect joy. . . . [T]his joy is inexpressible. . . . [I]t is called heaven which also signifies the heavenly society itself." In *Secrets of Heaven*, the loves are defined more specifically as "love for God and one's neighbor" *versus* "self-love and love for the world." There is a precedent for this definition of "loves" in *Hieroglyphic Key* §38 [proposition 4] and §39. Compare this with §46 about the doctrine of "ends" or "loves"; and with §31 about the absence of doctrine in the "beginning of creation" (referred to in *Secrets of Heaven* as the "earliest church").

18. The interplanetary scientist's frequency charts might be compared, in this regard, to a black-and-white photograph of a colored scene: one can observe in it subtle differences in tones of gray but has no way of translating them into the colors they reflect.

19. Quoted according to an interview with Brahms in the fall of 1896, as recorded in Abell 1964, 21.

20. Supporting evidence in this regard can be found in Swedenborg's later works as well; see, for example, *True Christianity* §12:8.

21. Contrary to the frequent mistranslation "animal kingdom" (suggesting the kingdom of the animals), *anima* refers to the human soul; that is to say, Swedenborg is speaking of the world of the (human) soul. On the Neoplatonic features in Swedenborg, see also Lang 2000, 28–33.

22. This is not to deny that Swedenborg sometimes refers to "causality" in the sense that spiritual realities are ultimately the origin of everything (see, for instance, *Secrets of Heaven* §§2993, 5711, 6048:2, 8211:2, 8812:5). My point here is that we are not dealing either with "instrumental" causality (as in natural mechanics) or with "occult causality" (where the cause somehow "beams down" or "transmits" invisible influences through space). The philosophical problem with notions of occult causality between soul and body is that one must assume the existence of some kind of "intermediate" substance or reality through which influences are transmitted.

23. This conclusion is found in *Hieroglyphic Key* §15 [correspondence 1] and would remain a constant in Swedenborg's visionary phase (see Williams-Hogan 1998, especially 220–222).

Chapter 2: The Structure of Secrets of Heaven, pp. 13–20

24. See Cole 1977 about Swedenborg's Hebrew Bible. In fact, Swedenborg seems to have used the bilingual Hebrew/Latin Bible published by Everard van der Hooght (1642?–1716) in 1740 (*Biblia Hebraica Secundum Editionem Belgii Edvardi Van der Hoogt, cum versione Latina Sebastian Schmidii*), which contained the Latin translation of Sebastian Schmidt (1617–1696) printed in parallel columns next to the Hebrew. Apart from that, he also used Schmidt's translation separately; Swedenborg's copy survives and is full of marginalia and underlinings. As demonstrated by Cole, there is no evidence for the claim of August Nordenskjöld (1754–1792) that Swedenborg "translated Genesis, Exodus, and the Apocalypse directly from the originals" (Nordenskjöld 1790, 87, as quoted in Cole 1977, 30).

25. To clarify the structure, I have subdivided the three strands. Titles have been added where necessary.

26. Section 1503 is missing.

27. Section 5396 was inadvertently repeated. The two paragraphs designated by that number are distinguished by the addition of *a* and *b* in the NEW CENTURY EDITION.

28. Section 7245 was inadvertently repeated. The two paragraphs designated by that number are distinguished by the addition of *a* and *b* in the NEW CENTURY EDITION.

29. Section 10175 was inadvertently repeated. The two paragraphs designated by that number are distinguished by the addition of *a* and *b* in the NEW CENTURY EDITION.

Chapter 3: Method, History, and Doctrine, pp. 21–36

30. The theoretical basis for this fundamental assumption is, of course, provided by the doctrine of correspondences as developed in the *Hieroglyphic Key*, as we have seen: "the principal matter must be expressed not by identical terms, but by different terms proper to each class . . . and, in fact, by terms which at first sight do not seem to signify or represent the same thing" (*Hieroglyphic Key* §4 [rules 2–3]).

31. This is one of several examples given by Swedenborg in *Secrets of Heaven* §1984. Later he devotes several sections to the sentence's inner meaning: §§6398–6401.

32. Swedenborg goes as far as saying that the Ten Commandments are unremarkable as far as the literal meaning is concerned: "the rules they lay down . . . are rules that non-Jews also acknowledge and have codified in their laws" (*Secrets of Heaven* §2609:1).

33. In his useful handbook to *Secrets of Heaven*, written from a Swedenborgian perspective, William F. Wunsch (1882–1969) made a point of denying that Swedenborg's method is allegorical (Wunsch 1929, especially chapter 5), claiming that his method does not entail a rejection of the literal meaning. There are problems with this assertion. First, as evidence of Swedenborg's view that "the sense of the letter (or Scripture as it stands and reads) is the sense from which any teaching for the guidance of Christian life is to be formulated, and on which it should be capable of being rested back" (Wunsch 1929, 20), Wunsch refers to a text written much later, around 1762: Swedenborg's unpublished manuscript *De Scriptura Sacra seu Verbo Domini ab Experientia*, variously referred to as *De Verbo*, *The Word from Experience*, or *Sacred Scripture*, as in Wunsch's case; and currently known as *Draft of "Sacred Scripture."* Wunsch admits that this explicit acceptance of the literal meaning is not found in *Secrets of Heaven* (Wunsch 1929, 20, note 11); therefore, it is most plausibly seen as evidence of a later change of opinion or emphasis on Swedenborg's part, which should not be projected backwards to the time when he wrote *Secrets of Heaven*. There is abundant evidence against Wunsch's view: see §§1874–1875 about the literal meaning of "dying away completely," which is presented as "purification"; and compare this with the preface that precedes §2760 ("what thick darkness people plunge into—dragging others with them—by interpreting everything literally" [*Secrets of Heaven* Genesis §22, preface:3]). Second, it is by no means as clear as suggested by Wunsch that the classic exponents of allegorical exegesis rejected the literal meaning. On this point, see Longenecker (1975, 29, 45–48) about the case of Philo of Alexandria (around 20 B.C.E.–50 C.E.).

34. But more complex subdivisions are common as well. Origen had distinguished between the literal, the moral, and the mystical sense. But the mystical sense could be divided further into allegorical and anagogical, leading to the four classic senses of Scripture. A frequently quoted example is the word *Jerusalem*: literally, it means a city; morally, it is a virtue; allegorically, it is the church; and anagogically, it is heaven. The division could be further complicated by dividing the literal sense into strictly his-

torical and figurative (see Williams 1948, 20; the classic study of the four senses of Scripture is de Lubac 1959).

35. See also the discussion in Lamm [1915] 2000, 224–237, especially 227.

36. I am referring to the formulation by Hans-Joachim Kraus (1982, 14) quoted earlier.

37. This, at least, is the general perspective that dominates *Secrets of Heaven*. It is, however, possible to find some passages (see for example §§4294, 4605–4609) that suggest a subdivision of further levels of meaning within the inner meaning.

38. When Swedenborg writes that these people were "with" him, he means that they were present with him in spiritual form. It is also worth noting that Swedenborg finds no value in historical research: "Viewed in themselves, however, the narratives do little to improve us. They have no effect at all on our eternal life, because in the other world historical detail is obliterated from memory" (§1886).

39. Third letter of Swedenborg to Beyer (Tafel 1877, 240–241). Swedenborg finishes the letter by pointing out that Paul's statements in 2 Romans 28, concerning justification by faith, have been misunderstood.

40. For this term (which is not used by Swedenborg himself), see Benz [1969] 2000, 452.

41. The distinction between heavenly and spiritual will be discussed in more detail below.

42. This is, of course, somewhat confusing: the "historical" parts are written in the "prophetical" style, but the contents are actually similar to those written in the style of the earliest church. These three styles are kept separate when Swedenborg speaks of our Bible but are here mixed together in his description of the lost Word of the ancient church.

43. *Secrets of Heaven* §3898:3. See also, for example, §2986.

44. Interestingly, Swedenborg discusses the development of the churches by means of a detailed exegesis of Matthew 24 (beginning with §3353 and ending with §4424).

45. *True Christianity* §779. See also Tafel 1877, 757.

46. Again, Swedenborg's discussions are sometimes confusing, and the framework given here is complicated by various factors, for example the fact that he sometimes uses the term *spiritual* in a broader sense (as in the next quotation in the text, from *Secrets of Heaven* §§7082–7083), some-

times in a more restricted sense (as when he uses *spiritual* as referring to a subdivision of love). My concern here is not to create a theological synthesis that harmonizes all variations in Swedenborg's terminology, but to present the general framework that structures his "teachings about Charity and Faith."

47. *Secrets of Heaven* §6705. See also §§7259–7260 for further information about these categories.

48. It would go beyond the scope of this discussion to go into the relation of this perspective with statements elsewhere in *Secrets of Heaven*, according to which will and intellect would nevertheless seem to have been separated after the flood (*Secrets of Heaven* §§310:1, 398, 640–641, 875:3–5, 895, 927:2, 933:4).

49. About this point, and on the entire doctrine of regeneration, see discussion in Lamm [1915] 2000, chapter 10, especially 266–274.

50. See also §8969.

Chapter 4: Biblical Exegesis, pp. 37–48

51. See also §1876.

52. Wunsch 1929, chapter 7, distinguishes three levels, by adding the dimension of "individual regeneration." Although the description of the Lord's development is certainly intended by Swedenborg as an ideal model to be emulated in the life of the individual, and at places can be read as referring to individual regeneration, it is clear already from Wunsch's own overviews (see especially chart 1 on page 129) that this third dimension is not an autonomous and independent one (it appears in Genesis 1, but this chapter is at the same time devoted to the "historical" dimension; and elsewhere it appears only occasionally within chapters devoted to the two other dimensions, and as "illustration" [Wunsch 1929, 46] of the Lord's life). Generally on the problems of Wunsch's charts, see Woofenden 1992.

53. On antisemitism in Swedenborg, see Hanegraaff 2004a.

54. Wunsch 1929, 57–69, links the stories of Abraham, Isaac, Jacob, and Joseph quite directly to stages in the Lord's biography. While the broad outlines of this interpretation may be correct, I find the connection less clear-cut.

55. *Secrets of Heaven* §§1651–1756. See also §§2764–2869.

56. *Secrets of Heaven* §§1535–1618. See also §§1985–2116.

57. *Secrets of Heaven* §6636 and §6644. The interpretation of part [1] is explained further and at length in §§6637–6639; of [2] in §6640; of [3] in §§6641–6642; of [4] in §6643; of [5] in §§6645–6646; and of [6] in §§6647–6649.

58. *Secrets of Heaven* §940. See also §7184: Reuben and Simon and their clans represent elements of faith; Levi and his clans, elements of charity; Aaron and his clans, elements of theology; Moses, elements of divine law.

59. On these eleven rather than ten plagues, see Cole 1977, 31: in his van der Hooght/Schmidius Bible (see note 24), Swedenborg counted eleven rather than ten plagues, by including the turning of Aaron's rod into a water-serpent.

60. See also §9592.

61. Swedenborg makes that statement in each of the five "summary" parts of the last books of Exodus: §§10750, 10767, 10782, 10807, and 10832.

Chapter 5: Accounts of Memorable Occurrences, pp. 49–56

62. See Dole 2000, especially note 4. See also Wilkinson 1996, 62: "It sold miserably." These assessments have their source in a quite amusing passage in Swedenborg, *Spiritual Experiences*, §4422: "I received a letter saying that not more than four copies had been sold within 2 months, and when this was made known to the angels, they were indeed surprised, but they said that it must be left to the Providence of the Lord, and that it is such that it compels no one. . . . "

63. See Dole 2000, 1. The exception is *De Ultimo Judicio* (Last Judgment). Woofenden 2002, 88, points out that it "broke new ground theologically by its claim that the long-expected last judgment predicted in the Bible has already taken place in the spiritual world by the time this work was published." In this context, it is interesting to compare the passages in *Secrets of Heaven* about the Last Judgment (especially §§2117–2134, 4661–4664, 4807–4809), where it is interpreted as referring, rather, to the individual "judging himself" after death.

64. Of the 603 sections of *Heaven and Hell*, thirty-four are direct quotations from *Secrets of Heaven* (see the table of parallel passages in Swedenborg 2000, 503).

65. Note that §§4523–4534 and §§4622–4634 can be read as a summary version of the whole and amount to an ideal short introduction to Swedenborg's view of heaven and hell.

66. These passages can be seen as the seed of a complete book, *Delitiae Sapientiae de Amore Conjugiali* (Wisdom's Delight in Marriage Love; current English title: *Marriage Love*), published by Swedenborg in 1768.

67. On the universal human, see §§3624–3649, 3741–3750, 3883–3896, 4039–4055, 4218–4228, 4318–4331, 4403–4421, 4523–4534, 4622–4634, 4652–4660, 4791–4806, 4931–4953, 5050–5062, 5171–5190, 5377–5396, 5552–5573.

68. On spiritual influence and divine inflow, see §§6053–6058, 6189–6215, 6307–6327, 6466–6496, 6598–6626.

69. See §2996.

70. See §§1521, 3636, 3638. However, in §1529 we read that the Lord appears to heavenly angels in the third heaven as the sun, but to spiritual angels as the moon.

71. See Lamm [1915] 2000, 255 and following; Williams-Hogan 2000 (the latter author does not, however, conclude that Swedenborg's universal human is an example of Kabbalistic influence; rather, she emphasizes the importance of Neoplatonism).

72. The exception is Idel 1997, who briefly discusses Swedenborg in this context. On the tradition as such, see also Scholem 1977; Schäfer 1988.

73. Some examples of authors who in fact did draw that conclusion are Giovanni Pico della Mirandola ([1463–1494]; see Pico della Mirandola 1942, 380); Cornelius Agrippa ([1486–1535]; *De Occulta Philosophia* [The Occult Philosophy] vol. 3, chapter 13; see Agrippa 1992, 437–439); and Paracelsus ([1493–1541]; *Opus Paramirum* 1:2; see Paracelsus 1925, 94–95).

74. Swedenborg speaks of three heavens, inhabited by spirits, angelic spirits, and angels, further subdividing each of the three into heavenly and spiritual ones (see, for example, §459; but notice that elsewhere he seems to divide heaven into two parts: see §4931). At times, he treats these categories as somewhat fluent, sometimes using "angels" as shorthand for all three categories. The distinctions are important, and used consistently, but the essential point for him is that all inhabitants of heaven have originally lived as human beings on earth (see, for example, §1114: "Angels and spirits, or in other words human beings after death . . ."; §1880: "to speak gen-

erally of spirits and angels, who are all human souls living on after the death of their body"). The concept is at odds with traditional Jewish as well as Christian notions, mystical or otherwise, of the relation between angels and human beings; see the longer discussion in Hanegraaff 2004a, note 55.

75. Swedenborg's distinction of three categories in heaven, each again subdivided into spiritual and heavenly, in no way contradicts this, for the distinction between spirits, angelic spirits, and angels is not ontological but has to do merely with successive levels of spiritual attainment. As such, each of the three, or six, categories finds its counterpart among living human beings. A human being's spiritual orientation during life on earth is decisive for the category to which he or she gravitates after death.

76. See also §3356: "the other world contains no concept of space or time but of state instead."

77. For further confirmation of that point, see §3633.

78. See also §1274.

79. "I have not been allowed to see what form hell itself is in overall. I have only been told that in the same way that all heaven as a single entity resembles a single human being . . . so all hell as a single entity resembles a single devil and can be manifested as a likeness of a single devil" (*Heaven and Hell* §553; translated by George F. Dole).

80. On this point see also *Heaven and Hell* §544.

81. For good examples of this sharp dualism, see §§7178–7182, 7366–7377, 8033–8037.

82. *Secrets of Heaven* §§698, 1106–1113; see also §§4944, 4947.

83. See the concept of "hades" introduced by Johann Heinrich Jung-Stilling (1740–1817) in his *Theorie der Geister-Kunde* (1808), and taken up by Johann Friedrich von Meyer (1772–1849) in his Hades (von Meyer 1810; for an exhaustive study, see Fabry 1989).

Chapter 6: The Early Reception of Secrets of Heaven, pp. 59–65

84. Among the more important overviews, in whom most of these figures and many others are discussed, see Bergmann and Zwink 1988; Larsen et al 1988; Brock et al 1988.

85. See Benz 1947, 264: the theologian Philipp Matthäus Hahn (1739–1790) devoted large parts of his diary of 1766 to comments on Swe-

denborg, who was likewise studied by scholars and theologians like Reuss, Kies, Clemm, Fricker, Hartmann, and various people from the nobility. Benz even claims that "in the correspondence of Württembergian scholars and pietists in these years, Swedenborg's person and doctrine are one of the most frequently treated subjects."

86. The first complete German translation, by Johann Friedrich Immanuel Tafel (1796–1863), appeared only as late as 1845–1869. See Benz 1947 about a failed attempt by the publisher Johann Friedrich Hartknoch (the same one who had published Kant's *Träume*) during the 1780s to realize a German translation of *Secrets of Heaven*.

87. The first Swedenborg translations in French were made in Berlin, by French authors associated with the esoteric group that would later become known as the Illuminés d'Avignon (see Snoek 2005): Dom Antoine-Joseph Pernety (1716–1796) published *Les merveilles du ciel et de l'enfer et des terres planétaires et astrales* in 1782, Louis Joseph Bernard Philibert de Morveau (1738–1786) (known as Brumore) brought out his *Traité curieux des charmes de l'amour conjugal dans ce monde et dans l'autre* in 1784, and it was followed by Pernety's *La sagesse angélique sur l'amour divin et sur la sagesse divine* in 1786. All these translations were severely criticized by Swedenborgians for the liberties that they took with the original (see Sjödén 1985, ch. 2). When J.F.E. Le Boys des Guays (1794–1864) (see below) claimed that many of Swedenborg's works were already translated into French before the French Revolution, but had become "very rare or sold out," he must have been referring to Pernety's and Brumore's work. In 1788 followed a compilation taken from various works, by Jean François Daillant Delatouche (who may either have made the translations himself or have acted as coordinator and editor of translations made by others); it was published anonymously as *L'abrégé des ouvrages d'Emmanuel Swedenborg*. The *Abrégé* of 1788 has been described as "one of the most important events in the history of Swedenborgianism," not least because both Abbé Augustin Barruel's (1741–1820) refutation of the New Church and Balzac's references to Swedenborg are entirely dependent on this compilation. The first integral French translations after those by Pernety and Brumore appeared from 1819 to 1824; they were made by a freemason and librarian of the Royal Library at Versailles, J.P. Moët. Moët also translated *Secrets of Heaven* in its entirety, but this translation remained unpublished.

The manuscript was consulted by Le Boys des Guays—who severely criticized it—while he was working on his own translation that would finally be published from 1841–1889 (on all this, see Sjödén 1985, 23–35, 51–52, 65–71, 95–124; cf. also Wilkinson 1996, 112–116).

88. See, for example, *Divine Love and Wisdom* (1788) and *Divine Providence* (1790) (Dole 2003a, 8–9; 2003b, 6–7).

89. Cf. Jonsson 1999, 196–197. Interestingly, Hyde (1906, 200) describes one translation of excerpts from *Secrets of Heaven*, by J.D. Halldin, dated as early as 1784. In addition to English, French, German and Swedish, Hyde (1906, 189–190) lists manuscripts of translations into Russian dated between 1851 and 1863.

90. Anonymus 1750, 313–316. I am grateful to Dr. E. Zwink (Württembergische Landesbibliothek, Stuttgart) for getting me a photocopy of this review.

91. Ernesti 1760; see also the accurate English translation by Berninger and Acton, in Cuno 1947, 139–170. Note that, while Berninger and Acton provide an English translation of a German original by Cuno (Cuno 1858), the latter does not contain the text of the review itself but merely refers to it; Berninger and Acton therefore traced down and translated Ernesti's original of 1760, and inserted it into their translation of Cuno. See also the analysis in Williams-Hogan 1998, 229–231.

92. Ernesti 1760, quoted according to Berninger and Acton 1947, 147.

93. Reference to a famous poem by Ludwig Holberg (1684–1754), *The Subterranean Voyage of Nicholas Klimm* (1741).

94. Ernesti 1760, quoted according to Berninger and Acton 1947, 152–153.

95. A few years later, in the fourth volume of his *Theologische Bibliothek*, Ernesti writes that he knows "the personality and the name of the author," but "must not mention it"; and in his index of authors, he classed *Secrets of Heaven* under the "Anonymi" (Berninger and Acton 1947, 139).

96. Ernesti 1767, 874–875; here quoted according to the excellent translation in Berninger and Acton 1947, 167–168.

97. Anonymus [J. C. Cuno] 1771, 7. The concept of *spiritus familiaris*—which allows Swedenborg to debate in heaven with persons who are still alive—is explained on the same page.

Chapter 7: Friedrich Christoph Oetinger, pp. 67–85

98. For an overview of Christian theosophy, see Faivre 2000a, 3–48. On Oetinger, see Breymayer 2005.

99. For an excellent discussion of Oetinger's relation to Leibniz and Wolff, see Spindler 1984.

100. See the definitive critical edition in two volumes: Oetinger [1763] 1977. There is also an excellent illustrated introduction by Betz (2000). Among Oetinger's earlier writings, see especially *Aufmunternde Gründe zur Lesung der Schrifften Jacob Boehmens* (Cheering Reasons to Read the Writings of Jacob Boehme, 1731), *Inquisitio in sensum communem et rationem* (Investigation of the Common and Rational Sense, 1752), *Die Wahrheit des Sensus Communis* (The Truth of the Common Sense, 1753/1754), *Die güldene Zeit* (The Golden Age, 1759–1761), *Die Philosophie der Alten wiederkommend in der güldenen Zeit* (The Philosophy of the Ancients returning in the Golden Age, 1762).

101. I am referring here to the classic study of Zimmermann 1969–1979, especially vol. I, 19–38, on the connection between eclecticism and "hermeticism" in the eighteenth-century context. See o.c., 31 for Zimmermann's concept of a *vernünftige Hermetik*; and see also the recent discussion by Neugebauer-Wölk 1999a, 17–23.

102. See the critical edition (Oetinger [1765] 1979).

103. Oetinger, letter to the earl of Castel, as quoted in Benz 1947, 9–10.

104. The relevant documents are Oetinger's exchange of letters with Swedenborg himself, beginning in 1766 (first published in Clemm 1767; see further Tafel 1890, III, 1027–1061; Benz 1947, 111–114); his *Rechtfertigungsschrift* (Document of Self-justification) of 1767, published in Benz 1947, 291–308; *Kurzgefasste Grundlehre des wirtt. Prälaten Bengel . . .* (A Short Account of the Basic Doctrine of the Württembergian Prelate Bengel) and *Abhandlung, wie man die heil. Schrift lesen und die Thorheit Gottes weiser halten solle . . .* (Treatise on How One Should Read the Holy Scripture and Consider God's Foolishness Wiser Than . . . [etc.]), both published in 1769; *Reflexionen über Swedenborgs Schrift von den Erdcörpern und Planeten* (Reflections about Swedenborg's Work about the Earthly Bodies and the Planets); *Sammlung einiger Nachrichten, Herrn Emanuel Swedenborg und desselben vorgegebenen Umgang mit dem Geisterreich betreffend*

(Collection of Some Reports concerning Mr. Emanuel Swedenborg and His Alleged Association with the Realm of Spirits); the so-called *Schwedische Urkunden* (Swedish Records) and *Schreiben von einer angeblichen Vermittlung des Streites* . . . (Writing about an Alleged Settlement in the Battle . . .), all from 1770; *Beurtheilung der wichtigen Lehre von dem Zustand nach dem Tod* . . . (Assessment of the Important Doctrine of the After-Death State . . .) from 1771; and *Gespräch von dem Hohenpriesterthum Christi* . . . (Conversation about Christ's Office of High Priest . . .).

105. A major problem in investigating the influence of Swedenborg in Germany consists in the fact that Oetinger—often an extremely sloppy writer, as we have seen—does not provide the numbers of the paragraphs he is translating. Certain problems, such as, for example, the question of a Swedenborgian influence on the physiognomy of J. C. Lavater (1741–1801) (see discussion in chapter 9, below), cannot be solved until we have a systematic text-critical comparison between Oetinger's translations and Swedenborg's Latin original. Only on that foundation will it be possible to see which passages were available to German readers who did not have access to the Latin and establish how faithfully Oetinger renders the original. In any case, it is clear that in his translations Oetinger concentrated almost exclusively on the "accounts of memorable occurrences," not on the exegetical parts.

106. Not to be confused with "pantheism." While pantheism refers to the doctrine that God is all and all is God, panentheism means that God is in all and all is in God. The former doctrine therefore states that the two terms are interchangeable because they refer to the same thing; the latter doctrine, in contrast, does not conflate them.

107. Oetinger [1765] 1977, I, 11. The *ens penetrabile* (a "subtle" substance more material than spirit and more spiritual than matter) is a major subject of discussion in Oetinger's *Metaphysic in Connexion mit der Chemie* (Metaphysics in Connection with Chemistry) of 1771 (published under the name of his son: Oetinger, Halophilo Irenäo 1771).

108. See detailed account in Benz 1947, ch. IV. The official ban made reference to *"ein gegen die Religion und Theologie anstössiges Buch."* (A Book That Offends Religion and Theology).

109. See also Benz 1975, 58: *"une contradiction entre les visions de Swedenborg qui révèlent des réalités célestes, et son exégèse qui transforme ces réalités en idées abstraites"* (A contradiction between Swedenborg's visions, which

reveal heavenly realities, and his exegesis, which transforms these realities into abstract ideas). On page 55, Benz illustrates this with the example of how Swedenborg interprets the vision of the heavenly Jerusalem in the Book of Revelation: at this point, he argues, one would expect detailed visionary information about that city, but Swedenborg actually translates the biblical images into doctrinal concepts.

110. On this point, see the analysis by Williams-Hogan 1998, esp. 220–222.

111. See note 22.

112. Swedenborg's own experiences of "the Lord" manifesting himself in the form of a man do not contradict this: they should not be seen as concrete manifestations that would have been visible to others, had they been present, but as based upon the opening of his own inner vision.

113. See, for example, H. I. [actually, F. C.] Oetinger 1771, 13: "For God's works, if one studies them, help to understand Holy Scripture, and Holy Scripture helps to understand God's works."

114. Literally "signatures of things:" a technical term within the "hermetic" philosophy of nature linked to the name of Paracelsus. Like the Bible, the "Book of Nature" can be read by man if he learns how to interpret its secret language. God speaks to us in nature by means of "signatures:" discreet signs that convey a hidden meaning.

115. H. I. Oetinger 1771, 23. Cf. also o.c., 29, about the effects of Christ's resurrection on the signatures of things; and Oetinger [1776] 1999, I, 244: "Scripture does not use the word 'law of nature' at all, because Nature is fallen and therefore cannot provide a law."

116. While I believe that Oetinger's perception of Swedenborg in this regard was essentially correct, I will not here go into the complex discussion about whether Swedenborg can be characterized as a docetist or whether the presence in his work of "docetist tendencies" might be merely apparent. Those who wish to explore the issue further will be interested in the fascinating clash between Ernst Benz and Henry Corbin (1903–1978) documented in the French journal *Cahiers de l'Université de Saint Jean de Jérusalem* 2 (1975). In his article *"L'idée de la Jérusalem céleste"* (Benz 1975, 51–73), Benz pointed out more clearly than in any of his previous writings this fundamental difference between Swedenborg and Oetinger. In

an editorial postscript ([Corbin] 1975, 71–74), the editor and founder of the journal, Henry Corbin, felt compelled to correct this as a *"grave malentendu"* (a serious misunderstanding): Oetinger had misunderstood Swedenborg, and the problem would no doubt have been resolved if the two had been able to meet in person. Antoine Faivre has recently called attention to the significance of this clash of opinion, in which actually Corbin represented a docetist perspective found in Swedenborg as well as in Islamic Ismaelism, while Benz represented the incarnational perspective of Oetinger. Faivre points out, correctly in my view, that it was Corbin who misunderstood Oetinger: he interpreted the concept of *Geistleiblichkeit* in terms of his own celebrated concept of the *"Mundus Imaginalis,"* not realizing that the latter is actually based upon idealist docetist assumptions and would have been rejected by Oetinger as strongly as Swedenborg was rejected by him (Faivre 2000b, 96).

117. For an extensive discussion, see Griffero 1999.

118. See discussion in, for example, Zimmermann 1979, 353–354; Benz 1979, 268.

119. See the splendid analyses in Deghaye 1985.

120. Oetinger, *Evangelien-Predigten* I (Leonberg 1837), 360, here quoted according to Benz 1979, 269.

121. See, for example, Oetinger [1776] 1999, I, 33–34 (lemma "Antichrist").

122. Oetinger's expression *"ein Pferdscheuer Schrecken"* is untranslatable.

123. Cf. the quotation attributed to Hermes in the lemma *"Gottesfurcht;"* Oetinger's reference is to Johann Jakob Manget, *Bibliotheca chemica curiosa* II (1702), 415: *"Hermes liber de pietate et Philosophia, inquiens: Qui pius est, summe philosophatur: et sine Philosophia summe pius esse est impossibile."*

124. Oetinger, *Selbstbiographie*, as quoted in Benz 1947, 86 (cf. Oetinger, *Beurtheilungen*). Oetinger took revenge in his *Reflexionen* of 1770, claiming that the idealists are punished after death by having to live in a purely idealist heaven, in which, like latter-day Tantaluses, they are fed only on abstractions, while all "realities" move outside their grasp whenever they try to reach for them (see Benz 1947, 141–142). Quite amusing are the visions of a young lady Wippermännin immediately after Swedenborg's death. She reported that the angels found Swedenborg an important man,

but regretted that he had lost his way: he should not have separated the internal from the literal sense of Scripture. Swedenborg himself did not yet understand his error, but Oetinger's pupil Fricker (who had died as well) was now busy trying to convince him of the correct interpretation of scripture (Benz 1947, ch. XVIII).

125. Oetinger, *Kurzgefasste Grundlehre; Abhandlung*.

126. Oetinger [1776] 1999, 417 (In: *Anhang: "Was besonders in heiliger Offenbarung sinnbildlich oder nach dem klaren Ausdruck zu nehmen"*). Benz (1975, 60) quotes the same passage but incorrectly states that it comes from the lemma *"Leiblichkeit" (Corporalité)*. The *Wörterbuch* contains no lemma of that title.

127. See, for example, Brecht 1995, 255.

128. At the end of a list of his published works, printed after his *De amore conjugiali* (see Benz 1947, 202).

129. As we already saw among the examples I gave of Swedenborg's "coding system," all of them taken from *Secrets of Heaven*. Swedenborg made the point very clearly in *Vera christiana religio*, but Oetinger might already have found it, for example, in *Arcana Coelestia*, Prefaetio before §2135.

130. Swedenborg, *Vera christiana religio* §779.

131. Johann Adam Osiander (1622–1697), a colleague of Oetinger.

132. On Oetinger's concept of *theologia emblematica*, its Dutch backgrounds, and its intimate connection with *Geistleiblichkeit* and a concrete-literalist understanding of Scripture, see Breymayer 1978, 1999.

133. Oetinger to Hartmann, February 1769, as quoted in Benz 1947, 109.

134. Oetinger [1776] 1999, 425. For the other Swedenborg references, see o.c., 69, 93, 111, 252–253, 301, 303.

Chapter 8: Immanuel Kant, pp. 87–107

135. However, among the abundant literature one finds much second-rate material that merely rehashes well-known facts. Among the contributions that offer something substantial or original are Vaihinger 1881 and 1892; Fischer 1898, 262–290; Delacroix 1904; van Os 1937; Ebbinghaus 1968; Courtès 1977; Jalley-Crampe 1979; Heinrichs 1979; Kirven 1988;

David-Ménard 1990; Florschütz 1992; Laywine 1993; Griffero 1997; and (especially important) Johnson 1996, 2001, 2002. A collective volume on Kant and Swedenborg, edited by Friedemann Stengel, is in preparation (title and publisher not yet known).

136. See examples in Hanegraaff forthcoming. A characteristic recent example is Schönfeld 2000. Having compared Kant's polemics with those of Fichte against Schmid, Hegel against Fries and the Romantics, and Marx/Engels against Bruno Bauer, Schönfeld writes that "what distinguished the polemics of the *Dreams* from these other works is that Kant did not assail a philosopher or theologian, but a mystic and assessor at the Swedish board of mines. His target was not an otherwise respectable theory, but a dreadful concoction of the fantastic and the occult" (2000, 235). Apparently Schönfeld is not aware of Swedenborg's international fame as a scientist and natural philosopher and considers himself excused from investigating the works of what he later refers to as "a self-styled magician." Not surprisingly, given such qualifications, Schönfeld's knowledge about Swedenborg turns out to be based upon second-hand accounts (primarily Laywine 1993); and from his overview of "the various available interpretations" of *Dreams* (2000, 238), one has to conclude that he has not taken the trouble to check any of the readily available critical studies of Swedenborg, such as those by Lamm or Jonsson. In other cases, for example in Kuehn's major biography of Kant (Kuehn 2001), the discussion of *Träume* is disappointingly superficial and simply does not address the question of why Kant found it important to devote a book to Swedenborg.

137. My respect for Johnson's work notwithstanding, I believe there are some problems with it. I find his translations not always beyond reproach (some examples will be mentioned in my notes), and I will contest his conclusions regarding Kant's later lectures on metaphysics. Another point, which I will not explore here, is that in discussing the relation between Kant and Swedenborg, Johnson often refers to Swedenborgian ideas that were developed by Swedenborg in his later works but are not yet to be found in *Secrets of Heaven* and which, therefore, did not play a role in Kant's criticism.

138. The original of the letter is no longer extant. Its contents were published by Ludwig Ernst Borowski (1740–1831) as an appendix to his Kant

biography of 1804 and are reprinted as appendices to the editions of *Träume* by Reich (Kant [1766] 1975, 71–76) and Malter (Kant [1766] 1976b, 99–106). An English translation is now available in Johnson 2002, 67–72. For earlier debates about the correctness of the date "1763," see the detailed discussion in Benz 1947, 241–271; additional and definitive proof is presented in Johnson 2002. To my knowledge, Courtès 1977 remains unique in believing the letter to be a forgery.

139. The translation "arch-visionary among all visionaries" (Johnson 2000, 42) sounds much more positive than the German *"phantast"* (here translated as "dreamer"), which has strong pejorative connotations.

140. It is possible that Kant always insisted on miswriting Swedenborg's name (perhaps in an attempt to Germanize it?), and that Borowski tacitly emended the spelling in transcribing the letter to Knobloch. In any case, by 1766, Kant certainly knew how to write Swedenborg's name; therefore, the misspelling was probably intentional and reflected the state of irritation so evident from his book. For the other differences, see text.

141. See Johnson 1996. The fragments are not Kant's own writings but give his ideas as interpreted by his students as well as by subsequent copyists and editors. They were written down amidst the jostle and distraction of a crowded lecture hall, and their quality depends on the level of the student in question. Kant considered his lectures not as occasions to teach his own philosophy, but as occasions to teach his students how to philosophize; therefore, it is often difficult to determine whether the views discussed are Kant's own. And finally, the notes record only the sequence of topics, but do not indicate the kind of relationships Kant established between them.

142. See note 139.

143. Hamann to Mendelssohn, in Kant [1766] 1976b, 111; Johnson 2002, 113.

144. This is further confirmed by Kant's letter to Mendelssohn of April 8, 1766 (see Kant [1766] 1976b, 113; Johnson 2002, 83–86).

145. As pointed out by Geier (2003, 106), Horace Walpole's *Castle of Otranto*—generally considered the beginning of the genre of the gothic novel—appeared in 1764.

146. The notion of a "subtle matter" that is both spirit and matter (as in Oetinger's notion of *Geistleiblichkeit*) is implicitly excluded.

147. Kant first argues that, thinking along these lines, there is no good argument why his soul could not be a material thing. If so, Leibniz's jesting idea that in drinking our coffee we might be devouring atoms that one day could become human souls might actually be no laughing matter. He continues: "But, in such a case, would this thinking 'I' not be subject to the common fate of material natures, and, just as by accident it was drawn from the chaos of all elements in order to animate an animal machine, why should it not also, after this accidental combination has dissolved, return to it again in the future?" Kant makes clear that this should not be understood as an argument in favor of reincarnation, but as a warning against this type of speculation: "It is sometimes necessary to startle a thinker who is on the incorrect path with the consequences [of his thought], so that he pays closer attention to the principles through which he has allowed himself to be led on as if in a dream."

148. Kant [1766] 1976b, 40. Johnson translates *Empfindung* as "sense"; I prefer "experience" because the German word may also refer to feeling or emotion.

149. Johnson, who tends to translate clearly pejorative terms by neutral or positive ones, translates *Wahnsinn* as "delusion." To translate *Verrückung* as "derangement" may be possible, and is in line with Kant's statement that it is a "higher state" of madness; but it is more commonly translated as a state of trance or ecstasy.

150. As early as 1898, Kuno Fischer called attention to the relevance in this respect of Kant's *Versuch über die Krankheiten des Kopfes* of 1764 (Kant [1764] 1960); for a study of Kant's *Träume* with a special focus on his ideas about madness, see David-Ménard 1990.

151. Kant is referring to the famous satire *Hudibras* written by Samuel Butler (1612–1680), which contains the following lines: "As wind in th'Hypocondries pent / Is but a blast if downwards sent; / But if it upwards chance to fly / Becoms [sic] new Light and Prophecy" (here quoted according to Johnson 2002, 172).

152. See note 4.

153. See, however, the strangely ambiguous sentences devoted to this aspect by Kuehn (2001, 174–175): "It would be tempting to see in these conclusions the first, even if incompletely expressed, theoretical conse-

quences of Kant's revolution and rebirth, and perhaps that is precisely what they are. However, it would be easy to exaggerate the importance of the work. It does not represent a revolutionary break with the past. His theory remains essentially the same as before." In other words: the passage is perhaps revolutionary, but nevertheless it is not!

154. The German *Schlaraffenland* literally means "Land of Cockaigne" or "Land of Plenty"; Johnson's translation "fool's paradise" certainly catches the intent.

155. Cf. the introduction by Klaus Reich, who edited the *Träume* together with Kant's *Von dem ersten Grunde des Unterschiedes der Gegenden im Raume* of 1768 (Reich 1976). We will see that, in the later lectures on metaphysics, it is again always the non-spatial nature of the spiritual world that stands in the center of attention.

156. The *Träume* also ends with some reflections on morality, but it is hard to understand how Manfred Kuehn, in his Kant biography, can say that "the entire book may be read as an argument for a naturalistic foundation of morality and against founding morality on the hope of a better state in another life" (Kuehn 2001, 174). This is indeed what we find on the last pages, but we do not find it in the rest of the book. Kuehn's statement may have been influenced by Fischer's analysis in his standard work of 1898.

157. Herder, review in *Königsbergischen Gelehrten und Politischen Zeitungen*, 18. Stück (3 March 1766). See reprint in Kant [1766] 1976b, 118–124; English translation in Johnson 2002, 114–118.

158. For both letters see Kant [1766] 1976b, 111–117; English translation in Johnson 2002, 82–86.

159. Kant to Mendelssohn, reprinted in Kant [1766] 1976b, 114.

160. Ibid, 115.

161. Mendelssohn, review of Kant, in *Allgemeine Deutsche Bibliothek* 4:2 (1767), 281; reprinted in Kant [1766] 1976b, 118; English translation in Johnson 2002, 123.

162. The German has *"wenn er nicht durch ihn erst ein kleines System sich gebauet hätte."* Johnson leaves out the important words *"durch ihn"* (by him); *"erst"* could also be translated simply as "first," as done by Johnson, but it seems to me that my solution better catches the author's intention.

163. Feder, review of Kant, in *Compendium Historiae Litterariae novissimae Oder Erlangische gelehrte Anmerkungen und Nachrichten auf das Jahr*

1766, 21:39 (23 september 1766), 308–309; reprinted in Kant [1766] 1976b, 125–127, quotation on 126; English translation in Johnson 2002, 120–121. Johnson provides translations from two other reviews, both anonymous and published in 1767; in my view, they do not add much new, so I do not discuss them here.

164. See remarks in note 141.

165. Thus in the "Parow Anthropology" (1772–1773), "Anthropology" (1781–1782).

166. Kant, "Metaphysic L 1", excerpt, as translated in Johnson 2002, 89–93.

167. Cf. Johnson's interesting discussion about the interpretation of this passage (Johnson 1996): he claims that Kant here incorrectly imputes to Swedenborg the belief that spiritual realities can be intuited while embodied, although Swedenborg's more subtle opinion is correctly summarized in *Träume*. As summarized by Johnson: "Swedenborg in fact claimed that spiritual beings appear to us by directly affecting our minds, creating visions of sensuous realities which are only symbolically related to underlying spiritual realities; the inner spiritual meaning of these visions must then be recovered by an act of interpretation." Although I think that Johnson is right, I am not sure that Kant necessarily attached so much importance to the distinction.

168. Kant, "Metaphysik Mrongovius," excerpt, as translated in Johnson 2002, 95–96.

169. Misspelled as "Schwedenburg," but this must no doubt be ascribed to the student who wrote down the notes.

170. *"Fragment einer späteren Rationaltheologie nach Baumbach,"* as translated in Johnson 1997, and excerpted in Johnson 2002, 107.

171. See the unfortunately rather apologetic discussion in Johnson 1997.

172. Note that Kant never discusses Swedenborg's claims about a direct perception of heavenly realities among the members of the Earliest Church. Swedenborg would have agreed with Kant only as far as present-day humanity is concerned.

173. This point has been recognized by many scholars. Thus, for example, Delacroix 1904, 567: "He had begun to read [*Secrets of Heaven*], and under the babble of a singularly scholastic theosophy, he found a doctrine that he knew well and with which he had been raised; perhaps the affinity of official metaphysics with Swedenborg's theosophy has contributed

to his quickly growing aversion against it." See also Benz 1947, 267, 270; David-Ménard 1990, 73; Johnson 1996.

174. I am referring, of course, to Goya's famous etching *El sueno de la razon produce monstruos* (1797–1798).

175. In the following I am referring to Foucault 1971.

Chapter 9: Some Later Readers of Secrets of Heaven, pp. 109–114

176. Hamann to Scheffner, as quoted in Fischer 1898, 275–276.

177. Lavater 1769 (letter 11), 177, as quoted in Benz 1938, 157–158. A second, but shorter and less interesting reference is found in volume 3 of Lavater's book (see Benz 1938, 159).

178. *Secrets of Heaven* §§358, 607–608, 2988–2989, 3527, 3573, 4799, 5695, 7360–7361, 8247, 8249–8250.

179. Oetinger's translations are limited to volume 1 of the Latin edition, *Secrets of Heaven* 1–1885, and concentrate on the "accounts of memorable occurrences." The physiognomical discussions of §358 and §§607–608 belong to the exegetical parts. Benz's reference to a physiognomical passage in *Secrets of Heaven* §1119 (Benz 1938, 168) is incorrect: the passage is about breathing.

180. Furthermore, it is likely that Goethe had access to at least parts of *De coelo* (that is to say, *Heaven and Its Wonders and Hell*), which is likewise based upon materials from *Secrets of Heaven* (see on this point Morris 1899, 505).

181. See Goethe's letter to a friend: "Dear Steinauer, please buy Swedenborg's heavenly philosophy compared etc. for me. The book has been published by prelate Oetinger in octavo in German"; Goethe's copy is still in his library and was bound on August 16 of the same year (undated letter in WA IV.3, 115 [nr. 520], as quoted in Gaier 1984, 99).

182. It is well known that legends about Agrippa became part of the Faust legend as known to Goethe. Agrippa had a black dog, whom he called "monsieur" and who was suspected by popular legend of being the devil in disguise; this is undoubtedly the origin of Mephistopheles' approaching Faust in the shape of a black poodle in Goethe's drama. Agrippa had authored two famous books, one on the uncertainty and vanity of all human arts and sciences (Agrippa 1531) and another on the occult sciences

(Agrippa [1533] 1992). Faust's monologue begins with a bitter complaint about the vanity of all human knowledge, entirely in line with Agrippa's *De incertitudine*, and in a desperate attempt to find certain knowledge, he turns to magic. What could be more logical, then, than to assume that we see here a reflection of a similar turn that was assumed to have been made by Agrippa (incorrectly, by the way, for the much-discussed incompatibility between Agrippa's two books is only apparent; on this point and the critical debate, see Van der Poel 1997, especially chapters 4 and 5)?

183. On Strindberg and Swedenborg, see, for example, Stockenström 1988 (the letter is quoted on p. 144).

184. Hitchcock [1858] 2003. On Hitchcock and his significance, see Versluis 2001, 64–71.

185. Originally published in 1927 as *My Religion*; see revised ed. [1994] 2000.

186. Personal communication (March 2003) by Dr. Eugene Taylor, who has consulted James's copy.

187. One instructive example is the composer Arnold Schönberg. His revolutionary method of composition known as dodecaphony is inseparable from his concept of "musical space," which he presented with explicit reference to Swedenborg's ideas about the non-spatial nature of heaven. We know that Schönberg was fascinated by Balzac's *Séraphita*, which contains a few references to Swedenborg's non-spatial heaven (see Covach n.d., 15 and note 12); but while it is true that he could have found much more specific and suggestive discussions in Swedenborg's originals, to which he could have had access, for example, through his pupils Alban Berg (1885–1935) and Anton Webern (1883–1945) (their Swedenborgian interests are discussed in Moldenhauer 1980 and Gratzer 1993), it remains the case that there is no evidence that Schönberg in fact studied Swedenborg in the original, let alone that he studied *Secrets of Heaven* (cf. also Wörner 1970).

Epilogue, p. 115

188. As demonstrated in Hanegraaff 2004b.

BIBLIOGRAPHY

Abell, Arthur M. 1964. *Talks with Great Composers*. Garmisch-Partenkirchen: G. E. Schroeder.

Agrippa, Cornelius. 1531. *De Incertitudine et Vanitate scientiarum et artium, atque excellentia verbi Dei declamatio*. Antwerp.

———. [1533] 1992. *De Occulta Philosophia Libri Tres*. Edited by V. Perrone Compagni. Leiden, New York, Köln: E. J. Brill.

Balzac, Honoré de. [1832–1835] 1900. *Séraphita*. Vol. 25 of *Honoré de Balzac*. New York: Peter Fenelon Collier & Son.

Benz, Ernst. 1938. "Swedenborg und Lavater: Über die religiösen Grundlagen der Physiognomik." *Zeitschrift für Kirchengeschichte* 57:153–216.

———. 1947. *Swedenborg in Deutschland: F. C. Oetingers und Immanuel Kants Auseinandersetzung mit der Person und Lehre Emanuel Swedenborgs, nach neuen Quellen bearbeitet*. Frankfurt am Main: Vittorio Klostermann.

———. 1958. *Die christliche Kabbala : Ein Stiefkind der Theologie*. Zürich: Rhein-Verlag.

———. 1975. "L'idée de la Jérusalem céleste chez les kabbalistes chrétiens: F.–C. Oetinger fondateur de la theosophie chrétienne allemande." *Jérusalem la cité spirituelle* (*Cahiers de l'université Saint Jean de Jérusalem*) 2:51–73.

———. 1979. "Die Naturtheologie Friedrich Christoph Oetingers." In *Epochen der Naturmystik: Hermetische Tradition im wissenschaftlichen Fortschritt*, edited by Antoine Faivre and Rolf Christian Zimmermann. Berlin: Erich Schmidt. 256–277.

———. [1969] 2002. *Emanuel Swedenborg: Visionary Savant in the Age of Reason*. Translated by Nicholas Goodrick-Clarke. West Chester, Pa.: Swedenborg Foundation.

Bergmann, Horst. 1988. "Swedenborg und Lavaters *Physiognomische Fragmente*." In *Emanuel Swedenborg 1688–1772: Naturforscher und Kundiger der Überwelt*, edited by Horst Bergmann and Eberhard Zwink. Stuttgart: Württembergische Landesbibliothek. 121–127.

Bergmann, Horst, and Eberhard Zwink, eds. 1988. *Emanuel Swedenborg 1688–1772: Naturforscher und Kundiger der Überwelt. Zum Werk des gelehrten Naturforschers. Zu Werk und Einfluss des Visionärs und Theologen. Zur Wirkungsgeschichte eines Naturphilosophen.* Stuttgart: Württembergische Landesbibliothek.

Berlin, Isaiah. 1993. *The Magus of the North: J. G. Hamann and the Origins of Modern Irrationalism.* London: Fontana.

Betz, Otto. 2000. *Licht vom unerschaffnen Lichte: Die kabbalistische Lehrtafel der Prinzessin Antonia in Bad Teinach.* Originally published in 1996. 2nd ed. Metzingen: Sternberg.

Borowski, Ludwig Ernst. 1993. *Darstellung des Lebens und Charakters Immanuel Kants.* Originally published in 1804. In *Immanuel Kant: Sein Leben in Darstellungen von Zeitgenossen*, edited by Felix Gross. Darmstadt.

Brecht, Martin. 1995. "Der württembergische Pietismus." In *Der Pietismus im achtzehnten Jahrhundert*, edited by Martin Brecht and Klaus Deppermann. Göttingen: Vandenhoeck & Ruprecht.

Breymayer, Reinhard. 1978. "Zu Friedrich Christoph Oetingers Theologia Emblematica und deren Niederländischen Wurzeln." In *Pietismus und Reveil*, edited by J. van den Berg and J. P. van Dooren. Leiden: E. J. Brill. 253–281.

———. 1995. "*Elias Artista*: Johann Daniel Müller aus Wissenbach/ Nassau, ein kritischer Freund Swedenborgs, und seine Wirkung auf die Schwäbischen Pietisten F. C. Oetinger und P. M. Hahn." In *Literatur und Kultur im deutschen Südwesten zwischen Renaissance und Aufklärung*, edited by Wilhelm Kühlmann. Amsterdam and Atlanta: Rodopi. 329–371.

———. 1999. "Friedrich Christoph Oetinger und die Emblematik." In *Biblisches und Emblematisches Wörterbuch*, by Friedrich Christoph Oetinger, edited by Gerhard Schäfer et al. Berlin and New York: Walter de Gruyter. Vol. II, 42–70.

———. 2005. "Oetinger, Friedrich Christoph." In *Dictionary of Gnosis and Western Esotericism*, edited by Wouter J. Hanegraaff et al. Leiden, etc.: E. J. Brill. 889–894.

Brock, Erland J., et al, eds. 1988. *Swedenborg and His Influence.* Bryn Athyn, Pa.: Academy of the New Church.

Clemm, Heinrich Wilhelm. 1767. *Vollständige Einleitung in die Religion und Gesammte Theologie.* Tübingen: Johann Georg Cotta.

Cole, Stephen. 1977. "Swedenborg's Hebrew Bible." *The New Philosophy* 80:28–33.

[Corbin, Henry]. 1975. "Note de la rédaction." *Jérusalem la cité spirituelle* (*Cahiers de l'université Saint Jean de Jérusalem*) 2:73–76.

Courtès, F. 1977. "Introduction: Le livre des dupes." In *Rêves d'un visionnaire*, by Immanuel Kant. Paris: Vrin. 7–44.

Covach, John. 1992. "Schoenberg and the Occult: Some Reflections on the 'Musical Idea.'" *Theory and Practice* 17:103–118.

[Cuno, J. C.]. 1771. *Sammlung einiger Nachrichten, Herrn Emanuel Swedenborg . . . und desselben vorgegebenen Umgang mit dem Geisterreich betreffend, nebst einem Schreiben an denselben, worinnen seine vornehmsten Meynungen geprüfet werden*. Hamburg: Herold.

Cuno, J.C. 1858. *Aufzeichnungen eines Amsterdamer Bürgers über Swedenborg. Nebst Nachrichten über den Verfasser*. Hannover: Carl Rümpler.

———. *J. C. Cuno's Memoirs on Swedenborg, to Which Is Added Dr. J. A. Ernesti's Libelous Attack and Its Refutation*. Translated by Claire E. Berninger and edited by Alfred Acton. Bryn Athyn, Pa.: Academy Book Room.

David-Ménard, Monique. 1990. *La folie dans la raison pure: Kant lecteur de Swedenborg*. Paris: Vrin.

Deghaye, Pierre. 1985. *La naissance de Dieu, ou la doctrine de Jacob Boehme*. Paris: Albin Michel.

———. 2000. "La notion de chair spirituelle chez Fr. Chr. Oetinger." In *De Paracelse à Thomas Mann: Les avatars de l'hermétisme allemand*. Paris: Dervy. 164–182.

Delacroix, Henri. 1904. "Kant et Swedenborg." *Revue de métaphysique et de morale* 12:559–578.

Dieckmann, Liselotte. 1970. *Hieroglyphics: The History of a Literary Symbol*. St. Louis, Mo.: Washington University Press.

Dole, George F. 2000. Translator's preface to *Heaven and Hell*, by Emanuel Swedenborg, translated by George F. Dole. West Chester, Pa.: Swedenborg Foundation. 1–6.

———. 2003a. Translator's preface to *Divine Love and Wisdom*, by Emanuel Swedenborg, translated by George F. Dole. West Chester, Pa.: Swedenborg Foundation. 1–10.

———. 2003b. Translator's preface to *Divine Providence*, by Emanuel
Swedenborg, translated by George F. Dole. West Chester, Pa.:
Swedenborg Foundation. 1–9.

Ebbinghaus, Julius. 1968. "Kant und Swedenborg." In *Gesammelte
Aufsätze, Vorträge und Reden*. Hildesheim: Georg Olms
Verlagsbuchhandlung. 58–79.

Ernesti, Johann August. 1760. Review of *Secrets of Heaven*, by Emanuel
Swedenborg. *Theologische Bibliothek* 1:515–527.

———. 1767. [about Swedenborg] in *Neue Theologische Bibliothek*
8:874–875.

Fabry, Jacques. 1989. *Le théosophe de Francfort Johann Friedrich von Meyer
(1772–1849) et l'ésotérisme en Allemagne au XIXe siècle*. 2 vols. Berne,
etc.: Peter Lang.

Faivre, Antoine. 1994. *Access to Western Esotericism*. Albany: State
University of New York Press.

———. 2000a. *Theosophy, Imagination, Tradition: Studies in Western
Esotericism*. Translated by Christine Rhone. Albany: State University
of New York Press.

———. 2000b. "La question d'un ésotérisme comparé des religions du
livre," in *Henry Corbin et le comparatisme spirituel* (*Cahiers du Groupe
d'Etudes Spirituelles Comparées*) 8:91–120. Paris: Archè-Edidit.

Feder, Johann Georg Heinrich. 1766. Review of *Dreams of a Spirit-Seer*,
by Immanuel Kant. *Compendium Historiae Litterariae Novissimae
Oder Erlangische gelehrte Anmerkungen und Nachrichten auf das Jahr
1766* 21:39 (September 23, 1766), 308–309.

Fischer, Kuno. 1898. *Immanuel Kant und seine Lehre*. Vol. 1. Heidelberg:
Carl Winter.

Florschütz, Gottlieb. 1992. *Swedenborgs verborgene Wirkung auf Kant:
Swedenborg und die okkulten Phänomene aus der Sicht von Kant und
Schopenhauer*. Würzburg: Königshausen & Neumann.

Foucault, Michel. 1971. *L'ordre du discours*. Paris: Gallimard.

Gaier, Ulrich. 1984. "Nachwirkungen Oetingers in Goethes Faust."
Pietismus und Neuzeit 10:90–123.

———. 1988. "'Könnt' ich Magie von meinem Pfad entfernen':
Swedenborg im magischen Diskurs von Goethes *Faust*." In *Emanuel
Swedenborg 1688–1772: Naturforscher und Kundiger der Überwelt*,

edited by Horst Bergmann and Eberhard Zwink. Stuttgart: Württembergische Landesbibliothek. 129–139.

Geier, Manfred. 2003. *Kants Welt: Eine Biographie*. Reinbek bei Hamburg: Rowohlt.

Goethe, Johann Wolfgang von. 1773. Review of *Aussichten in die Ewigkeit*, by Johann Caspar Lavater. *Frankfurter gelehrte Anzeigen* 37:261.

Gratzer, Wolfgang. 1993. *Zur "wunderlichen Mystik" Alban Bergs: Eine Studie*. Wien, Köln, Weimar: Böhlau Verlag.

Griffero, Tonino. 1997. "'Die Geisterwelt ist nicht verschlossen': Kant e Oetinger giudici di Swedenborg." *Rivista di estetica* 37, n.s. 5, 163–234.

——. 1999. "I sensi di Adamo: Appunti estetico-theosofici sulla corporeità spirituale." *Rivista di estetica* 39, n.s. 12:3, 119–225.

Hanegraaff, Wouter J. 1995. "Empirical Method in the Study of Esotericism." *Method and Theory in the Study of Religion* 7:99–129.

——. 1996–1998. *New Age Religion and Western Culture: Esotericism in the Mirror of Secular Thought*. Leiden, New York, Köln: E. J. Brill, and Albany: State University of New York Press.

——. 2001. "Beyond the Yates Paradigm: The Study of Western Esotericism Between Counterculture and New Complexity." *Aries* 1:5–37.

——. 2004a. "Emanuel Swedenborg, the Jews, and Jewish Traditions." In *Reuchlin und seine Erben: Forscher, Denker, Ideologen und Spinner*, edited by Peter Schäfer and Irina Wandrey. Ostfildern: Jan Thorbecke. 135–154.

——. 2004b. "Spectral Evidence of New Age Religion: On the Substance of Ghosts and the Use of Concepts." *Journal of Alternative Spiritualities and New Age Studies* 1:35–58.

——. 2004c. "The Study of Western Esotericism: New Approaches to Christian and Secular Culture." In *New Approaches to the Study of Religion*, edited by Peter Antes, Armin W. Geertz, and Randi Warne. Berlin and New York: De Gruyter. Vol. I, 489–519.

——. 2005. Entry for "Tradition." In *Dictionary of Gnosis and Western Esotericism*, edited by Wouter J. Hanegraaff et al. Leiden, etc.: E. J. Brill. 1125–1135.

——. 2007. "Swedenborg's *Magnum Opus.*" In Swedenborg, *Secrets of Heaven*, West Chester: Swedenbourg Foundation.

——. Forthcoming. "Swedenborg aus der Sicht von Kant und der akademischen Kant-Forschung." In collective volume on Kant and Swedenborg, edited by Friedemann Stengel (title and publisher not yet known).

Heinrichs, Michael. 1979. *Emanuel Swedenborg in Deutschland: Eine kritische Darstellung der Rezeption des schwedischen Visionärs im 18. und 19. Jahrhundert.* Frankfurt am Main: Peter D. Lang.

Henck, Herbert. 2001. "Vom Monochord zur vierten Dimension: Johann Ludwig Frickers irdische und himmlische Musik." *Neue Zeitschrift für Musik* 1:48–51.

Herder, Johann Gottfried von. 1766. Review of *Dreams of a Spirit-Seer*, by Immanuel Kant. *Königsbergischen Gelehrten und Politischen Zeitungen*, 18. Stück (March 3, 1766).

Hitchcock, Ethan Allen. [1858] 2003. *Swedenborg: A Hermetic Philosopher. An Interpretation of Emanuel Swedenborg's Writings from the Standpoint of Hermetic Philosophy, with a Study Comparing Swedenborg and Spinoza.* Charleston: Arcana Books.

Hooght, Everardus van der. 1740. *Biblia Hebraica Secundum Editione Belgicam Everardi van der Hooght, Collatis Aliis Bonae Notae Codicibus, Una cum Versione Latina Sebastiani Schmidii.* Leipzig: Wolfgang Deer.

Hyde, James. 1906. *A Bibliography of the Works of Emanuel Swedenborg, Original and Translated.* London: Swedenborg Society.

Idel, Moshe. 1997. "Il mondo degli angeli in forma umana." *Rassegna mensile d'Israel* 63:1–76. Hebrew original in *Jerusalem Studies in Jewish Thought*, edited by J. Dan and J. Hacker, Jerusalem, 1986, 1–66.

Israel, Jonathan. 2001. *Radical Enlightenment : Philosophy and the Making of Modernity 1650–1750.* Oxford: Oxford University Press.

——. *Enlightenment Contested: Philosophy, Modernity, and the Emancipation of Man 1670–1752.* Oxford: Oxford University Press.

Jalley-Crampe, Michèle. 1979. "La raison et ses rêves: Kant juge de Swedenborg." *Revue des sciences humaines* 176:9–21.

Johnson, Gregory R. 1996. "Kant on Swedenborg in the *Lectures on Metaphysics.* Part 1: 1760s–1770s." *Studia Swedenborgiana* 10(1):1–38.

———. 1997. "Kant on Swedenborg in the *Lectures on Metaphysics.* Part 2." *Studia Swedenborgiana* 10(2):11–39.

———. 2001. "A Commentary on Kant's *Dreams of a Spirit-Seer.*" Dissertation, Catholic University of America.

———, ed. 2002. *Kant on Swedenborg: "Dreams of a Spirit-Seer" and Other Writings.* West Chester, Pa.: Swedenborg Foundation.

Jonsson, Inge. 1969. *Swedenborgs Korrespondenslära.* Stockholm: Almqvist & Wiksell.

———. 1970. "Swedenborg's Doctrine of Correspondence." *The New Philosophy* 73:299–327.

———. 1979. "Emanuel Swedenborgs Naturphilosophie und ihr Fortwirken in seiner Theosophie." In *Epochen der Naturmystik: Hermetische Tradition im wissenschaftlichen Fortschritt,* edited by Antoine Faivre and Rolf Christian Zimmermann. Berlin: Eric Schmidt.

———. [1971] 1999. *Visionary Scientist: The Effects of Science and Philosophy on Swedenborg's Cosmology.* West Chester, Pa.: Swedenborg Foundation.

Jung, genannt Stilling, Heinrich. 1808. *Theorie der Geister-Kunde, in einer Natur-, Vernunft- und Bibelmässigen Beantwortung der Frage: Was von Ahnungen, Gesichten und Geistererscheinungen geglaubt und nicht geglaubt werden müsste.* Nürnberg: Raw'schen Buchhandlung.

Kant, Immanuel. [1755] 1995. *Allgemeine Naturgeschichte und Theorie des Himmels, oder Versuch von der Verfassung und dem mechanischen Ursprunge des ganzen Weltgebäudes, nach Newtonischen Grundsätzen.* In *Werke in sechs Bänden,* vol. I. Köln: Könemann. 5–189.

———. [1764] 1960. *Versuch über die Krankheiten des Kopfes.* In *Vorkritische Schriften bis 1768,* Frankfurt am Main: Insel Verlag. 887–901.

———. 1766. *Träume eines Geistersehers, erläutert durch Träume der Metaphysik.* Riga: Johann Friedrich Hartknoch.

———. [1766] 1975. *Träume eines Geistersehers/Der Unterschied der Gegenden im Raume.* Edited by Klaus Reich. Hamburg: Felix Meiner.

———. [1783] 1976a. *Prolegomena zu einer jeden künftigen Metaphysik.* Edited by Karl Vorländer. Hamburg: Felix Meiner.

———. [1766] 1976b. *Träume eines Geistersehers, erläutert durch Träume der Metaphysik.* Edited by Rudolf Malter. Stuttgart: Reclam.

Keller, Helen. [1994] 2000. *Light in My Darkness.* Edited by Ray Silverman. West Chester, Pa.: Swedenborg Foundation.

Kirven, Robert H. 1988. "Swedenborg and Kant Revisited: The Long
    Shadow of Kant's Attack and a New Response." In *Swedenborg and
    His Influence*, edited by Erland J. Brock et al. Bryn Athyn, Pa.:
    Academy of the New Church. 103–120.

Kraus, Hans-Joachim. 1982. *Geschichte der historisch-kritischen
    Erforschung des Alten Testaments*. 3rd expanded ed. Neukirchen-
    Vluyn: Neukirchener Verlag.

Kuehn, Manfred. 2001. *Kant: A Biography*. Cambridge: Cambridge
    University Press.

Lamm, Martin. [1915] 2000. *Emanuel Swedenborg: The Development of
    His Thought*. Translated by Tomas Spiers and Anders Hallengren.
    West Chester, Pa.: Swedenborg Foundation.

Lang, Bernhard. 2000. "On Heaven and Hell: A Historical Introduction
    to Swedenborg's Most Popular Book." In *Heaven and Its Wonders
    and Hell*, by Emanuel Swedenborg, translated by George F. Dole.
    West Chester, Pa.: Swedenborg Foundation. 9–64.

Larsen, Robin, et al, eds. 1988. *Emanuel Swedenborg: A Continuing
    Vision. A Pictorial Biography and Anthology of Essays and Poetry*. New
    York: Swedenborg Foundation.

Lavater, Johann Caspar. 1769. *Aussichten in die Ewigkeit, in Briefen an
    Herrn Joh. Georg Zimmermann*. Vol. 2. Zürich: Orell, Gessner und
    Comp.

Laywine, Alison. 1993. *Kant's Early Metaphysics and the Origins of the
    Critical Philosophy*. North American Kant Society Studies in
    Philosophy 3. Ridgeview: Atascadero, Calif.

Longenecker, Richard. 1975. *Biblical Exegesis in the Apostolic Period*.
    Grand Rapids, Mich.: William B. Eerdmans.

Lubac, Henri de. 1959. *Exégèse médiévale: Les quatre sens de l'Écriture*.
    Paris: Aubier.

Lütgert, Wilhelm. 1923. *Die Religion des deutschen Idealismus und ihr
    Ende*. Vol. 1. Gütersloh: C. Bertelsmann.

Mälzel, Gottfried. 1970. *Johann Albrecht Bengel: Leben und Werk*.
    Stuttgart: Calwer.

Manget, Johann Jakob. 1702. *Bibliotheca Chemica Curiosa*. Vol. 2.
    Geneva: Chouet.

Mendelssohn, Moses. 1767. Review of *Dreams of a Spirit-Seer*, by
    Immanuel Kant. *Allgemeine Deutsche Bibliothek* 4:281.

Meyer, Johann Friedrich von. 1810. *Hades: Ein Beytrag zur Theorie der Geisterkunde. Nebst Anhängen: öffentliche Verhandlungen über Swedenborg und Stilling, ein Beyspiel des Ahnungsvermögens und einen Brief des jüngeren Plinius enthaltend.* Frankfurt am Main: J. C. Hermann.

Moldenhauer, Hans, and Rosaleen Moldenhauer. 1980. *Anton von Webern: Chronik seines Lebens und Werkes.* Zürich, Freiburg im Breisgau: Atlantis.

Morris, Max. 1899. "Swedenborg im Faust." *Euphorion* 6:491–510.

Neugebauer-Wölk, Monika. 1999a. "Esoterik im 18. Jahrhundert-Aufklärung und Esoterik. Eine Einleitung." In *Aufklärung und Esoterik*, edited by Monika Neugebauer-Wölk. Hamburg: Felix Meiner. 1–37.

———, ed. 1999b. *Aufklärung und Esoterik.* Hamburg: Felix Meiner.

———. 2000. "Esoterik in der frühen Neuzeit: Zum Paradigma der Religionsgeschichte zwischen Mittelalter und Moderne." *Zeitschrift für historische Forschung* 27:321–364.

———. 2003. "Esoterik und Christentum vor 1800: Prolegomena zu einer Bestimmung ihrer Differenz." *Aries* 3:127–165.

Nordensköld, August. 1790. "Remarks by Mr. A. N. on the Different Editions of the Bible Made Use of by Emanuel Swedenborg." *New-Jerusalem Magazine* 1:87–88.

Oetinger, Friedrich Christoph. [1765] 1977. *Swedenborgs und anderer irdische und himmlische Philosophie zur Prüfung des Besten ans Licht gestellt.* 2 parts. Ed. K.C.E. Ehmann 1858; facsimile reprint as *Swedenborgs irdische und himmlische Philosophie* (ed. E. Beyreuther) in Oetinger, *Sämtliche Schriften* 2. Abt., 2 Bd., J. F. Steinkopf: Stuttgart 1977.

———. [1763] 1977. *Die Lehrtafel der Prinzessin Antonia.* Edited by Reinhard Breymayer and Friedrich Häussermann. Texte zur Geschichte des Pietismus Abt. VII, Bd. 1. 2 vols. Berlin and New York: Walter de Gruyter.

———. [1765] 1979. *Theologia ex Idea Vitae Deducta.* Edited by Konrad Ohly. Texte zur Geschichte des Pietismus Abt. VII, Bd. 2. 2 vols. Berlin and New York: Walter de Gruyter.

———. [1776] 1999. *Biblisches und Emblematisches Wörterbuch.* Edited by Gerhard Schäfer et al. Texte zur Geschichte des Pietismus Abt. VII, Bd. 3. 2 vols. Berlin and New York: Walter de Gruyter.

Oetinger, Halophilo Irenäo. 1771. *Die Metaphysic in Connexion mit der Chemie, worinnen sowohl die wichtigste übersinnliche Betrachtungen der Philosophie und Theologiae Naturalis & Revelatae, als auch ein clavis und Select aus Zimmermanns und Neumanns allgemeinen Grundsätzen der Chemie nach den vornehmlichen subjectis in alphabetischer Ordnung nach Beccheri heut zu Tag recipirten Gründen abgehandelt werden, samt einer Dissertation de Digestione, ans Licht gegeben von Halophilo Irenäo Oetinger, Medicinae Licentiato und Philos. Hermeticae cultore.* Schwäbisch Hall n.d.

Os, C. H. van. 1937. "Swedenborg en Kant." *Synthese: Maandblad voor het geestesleven van onzen tijd.* 514–526.

Paracelsus. 1925. *Medizinische, naturwissenschaftliche und philosophische Schriften.* Edited by Karl Sudhoff. Vol. 9, *"Paramirisches" und anderes Schriftwerk der Jahre 1531–1535 aus der Schweiz und Tirol.* München and Planegg: Barth.

Pico della Mirandola, Giovanni. 1942. *De Homine Dignitate, Heptaplus, De Ente et Uno.* Edited by Eugenio Garin. Florence: Vallecchi.

Poel, Marc van der. 1997. *Cornelius Agrippa: The Humanist Theologian and His Declamations.* Leiden, New York, Köln: E. J. Brill.

Reich, Klaus. 1975. "Kants Behandlung des Raumbegriffs in den *Träumen eines Geistersehers* und im *Unterschied der Gegenden im Raum.*" In *Träume eines Geisterseher/Der Unterschied der Gegenden im Raume,* edited by Klaus Reich. Hamburg: Felix Meiner. V–XVIII.

Review of *Secrets of Heaven,* by Emanuel Swedenborg. 1750. *Neue Zeitungen von Gelehrten Sachen* 36:313–316.

Review of *Swedenborg's and Others' Earthly and Heavenly Secrets,* by Friedrich Christof Oetinger. 1766. *Göttinger Anzeigen von gelehrten Sachen* 26–27:201 and following.

Roling, Bernd. 2006. "Erlösung im angelischen Makrokosmos: Emanuel Swedenborg, die *Kabbala denudata* und die schwedische Orientalistik." *Morgen-Glantz* 16:385–457.

Schäfer, Peter. 1988. "*Shi'ur Qoma*: Rezensionen und Urtext." In *Hekhaloth-Studien.* Tübingen: J.C.B. Mohr (Paul Siebeck).

Schmidt, Sebastian, trans., and Emanuel Swedenborg, annotator. 1872. *Biblia Sacra sive Testamentum Vetus et Novum ex Linguis Originalibus in Linguam Latinam Translatum . . . Annotationibus Emanuelis Svedenborgii Manu Scriptis Locupletati. . . .* Edited by R. L. Tafel. Stockholm: Photolithographic Society.

Scholem, Gershom. [1937] 1979. "A Birthday Letter from Gershom Scholem to Zalman Schocken." In David Biale, *Gershom Scholem: Kabbalah and Counter-History*, Cambridge, Mass. & London: Harvard University Press. 215–216.

Scholem, Gershom. 1977. "*Schi'ur Koma*: Die mystische Gestalt der Gottheit." In *Von der mystischen Gestalt der Gottheit: Studien zu Grundbegriffen der Kabbala*. Frankfurt am Main: Suhrkamp. 7–47.

Schönfeld, Martin. 2000. *The Philosophy of the Young Kant: The Precritical Project*. Oxford: Oxford University Press.

Schuchard, Marsha Keith. 1995. "Yeats and the 'Unknown Superiors': Swedenborg, Falk, and Cagliostro." In *Secret Texts: The Literature of Secret Societies*, edited by Marie Mulvey Roberts and Hugh Ormsby-Lennon. New York: AMS Press. 114–168.

———. 1998. "Leibniz, Benzelius, and the Kabbalistic Roots of Swedish Illuminism." In *Leibniz, Mysticism and Religion*, edited by Allison P. Coudert, Richard H. Popkin, and Gordon M. Weiner. Dordrecht, Boston, London: Kluwer Academic Publishers. 84–106.

———. 1999. "Emanuel Swedenborg: Deciphering the Codes of a Celestial and Terrestrial Intelligencer." In *Rending the Veil: Concealment and Secrecy in the History of Religions*, edited by Elliott R. Wolfson. New York, London: Seven Bridges Press. 177–207.

———. 2001. "Dr. Samuel Jacob Falk: A Sabbatian Adventurer in the Masonic Underground." In *Millenarianism and Messianism in Early Modern European Culture: Jewish Messianism in the Early Modern World*, edited by M. D. Goldish and R. H. Popkin. Dordrecht, Boston, London: Kluwer Academic Publishers. 203–226.

[Sewall, Frank.] 1906. "Swedenborg's Influence upon Goethe." *The New Philosophy* 9:12–26.

Sjödén, Karl-Erik. 1985. *Swedenborg en France*. Edsbruk: Almqvist & Wiksell.

Snoek, J.A.M. 1995. "Similarity and Demarcation." In *Pluralism and Identity: Studies in Ritual Behaviour*, edited by Jan Platvoet and Karel van der Toorn. Leiden etc.: E. J. Brill.

——. 2005. "Illuminés d'Avignon." In *Dictionary of Gnosis and Western Esotericism*, edited by Wouter J. Hanegraaff et al. Leiden, etc.: E. J. Brill. 597–600.

Spindler, Guntram. 1984. "Oetinger und die Erkenntnislehre der Schulphilosophie des 18. Jahrhunderts." *Pietismus und Neuzeit* 10:22–65.

Stockenström, Göran. 1988. "Strindberg and Swedenborg." In *Emanuel Swedenborg: A Continuing Vision*, edited by Robin Larsen et al. New York: Swedenborg Foundation. 137–158.

Stuckrad, Kocku von. 2005. *Western Esotericism: A Brief History of Secret Knowledge*. London / Oakville: Equinox.

Swedenborg, Emanuel. 1734. *Prodromus Philosophiae Ratiocinantis de Infinito, et Causa Finali Creationis*. Dresden and Leipzig: Frederick Hekel.

——. 1740–1741. *Oeconomia Regni Animalis in Transactiones Divisa*. 2 vols. Amsterdam: François Changuion. English version: *The Economy of the Animal Kingdom Considered Anatomically, Physically, and Philosophically*, 2 vols., translated by Augustus Clissold. Bryn Athyn, Pa: Swedenborg Scientific Association, 1955. First edition of the English translation: 1845, London: W. Newbery, H. Bailliere.

——. 1749–1756. *Arcana Coelestia, Quae in Scriptura Sacra, seu Verbo Domini Sunt, Detecta*. 8 vols. [London: John Lewis.]

——. 1750. *Secrets of Heaven*. Vol. 2. Translated by John Marchant. [London: John Lewis.]

——. 1758a. *De Equo Albo, de Quo in Apocalypsi, Cap. XIX: Et Dein de Verbo et Ejus Sensu Spirituali seu Interno, ex Arcanis Coelestibus*. London: [John Lewis.]

——. 1758b. *De Telluribus in Mundo Nostro Solari, Quae Vocantur Planetae, et de Telluribus in Coelo Astrifero, deque Illarum Incolis, Tum de Spiritibus et Angelis Ibi: Ex Auditis et Visis*. London: [John Lewis.]

——. 1758c. *De Ultimo Judicio, et de Babylonia Destructa: Ita Quod Omnia, Quae in Apocalypsi Praedicta Sunt, Hodie Impleta Sunt: Ex Auditis et Visis*. London: [John Lewis.]

——. 1768. *Delitiae Sapientiae de Amore Conjugiali*. Amsterdam.

——. [1758] 1770. *Von den Erdcörpern der Planeten*. Translated by Friedrich Christoph Oetinger. N.p.

——. [1758] 1778. *A Treatise Concerning Heaven and Hell*. Translated by William Cookworthy and Thomas Hartley. London: James Phillips.

———. [1758] 1782. *Les merveilles du ciel et de l'enfer et des terres planétaires et astrales.* Translated by Antoine-Joseph Pernety. Berlin: G. J. Decker.

———. 1783–1806. *Arcana Coelestia: or Heavenly Mysteries.* 12 vols. Translated by John Clowes. London: R. Hindmarsh (vols. 1–8), J. Hodson (vols. 8–10), J. and E. Hodson (vols. 11–12).

———. 1784a. *Clavis Hieroglyphica Arcanorum Naturalium et Spiritualium, per Viam Repraesentationum et Correspondentiarum.* London: Robert Hindmarsh.

———. 1784b. *Traité curieux des charmes de l'amour conjugal dans ce monde, et dans l'autre.* Translated by [de] Brumore (Louis Joseph Bernard Philibert de Morveau). Berlin and Basel: George-Jacques and J. Henri Decker.

———. 1786. *La sagesse angélique sur l'amour divin et sur la sagesse divine.* 2 vols. Translated by Antoine-Joseph Pernety. Lyons.

———. 1788. *Abrégé des Ouvrages d'Ém. Swédenborg.* Prepared by Jean François Daillant de la Touche. Stockholm [Strasbourg]: Exegetical and Philanthropical Society.

———. 1792. *An Hieroglyphic Key to Natural and Spiritual Mysteries, by Way of Representations and Correspondences.* Translated by Robert Hindmarsh. London: R. Hindmarsh.

———. 1821. *Himmelska lönnligheter.* 3 vols. Translated by J. Tybeck and J. A. Sevén. Stockholm: Pro Fide et Charitate. This Swedish translation of *Secrets of Heaven* extended only as far as §3649.

———. 1841–1854. *Arcanes célestes.* 16 vols. Translated by Jean-François-Étienne Le Boys des Guays. Saint-Amand (Cher): Librairie de *La Nouvelle Jérusalem.*

———. 1845–1869. *Himmlische Geheimnisse.* Translated by J.F.I. Tafel. 16 vols. Tübingen: Verlags-Expedition.

———. 1847. *A Hieroglyphic Key to Natural and Spiritual Mysteries, by Way of Representations and Correspondences.* Translated by James John Garth Wilkinson. London: William Newbery, and Boston: Otis Clapp.

———. 1916–1917. "A Hieroglyphic Key to Natural and Spiritual Arcana by Way of Representations and Correspondences." [Translated by Alfred Acton.] *The New Philosophy* 19:305–319; 20:32–52.

———. [1734] 1954. *Principia Rerum Naturalium sive Novorum Tentaminum Phaenomena Mundi Elementaris Philosophice Explicandi.*

Basel: Swedenborg Institut. Facsimile of first volume of 1734 edition, Dresden and Leipzig: Frederick Hekel. English version: *The Principia; or, The First Principles of Natural Things*, 2 vols., translated by Augustus Clissold, Bryn Athyn, Pa.: Swedenborg Scientific Association, 1988. First edition of this translation: 1846, London: W. Newbery.

——. 1984. "Hieroglyphic Key to Spiritual and Natural Arcana." In *Psychological Transactions and Other Posthumous Tracts 1734–1744*. Translated by Alfred Acton. 2nd ed. Bryn Athyn, Pa.: Swedenborg Scientific Association.

——. [1770] 1996. *The Natural and Spiritual Sense of the Word*. In vol. 2 of *Posthumous Theological Works*, translated by John Whitehead and edited by William Ross Woofenden. West Chester, Pa.: Swedenborg Foundation.

——. 1997. *The Sacred Scripture or Word of the Lord from Experience*. In *Three Short Works*, translated by N. Bruce Rogers. Bryn Athyn, Pa.: General Church of the New Jerusalem.

——. 1998–2002. *Emanuel Swedenborg's Diary, Recounting Spiritual Experiences during the Years 1745 to 1765*. 3 vols. Translated by J. Durban Odhner. Bryn Athyn, Pa.: General Church of the New Jerusalem. The first three volumes, in English, of the six volumes of Swedenborg's Latin work *Experientiae Spirituales*, edited by J. Durban Odhner (Bryn Athyn, Pa.: Academy of the New Church, 1983–1997). Further volumes forthcoming.

——. 2000. *Heaven and Its Wonders and Hell, Drawn from Things Heard and Seen*. Translated by George F. Dole, with an introduction by Bernhard Lang. West Chester, Pa.: Swedenborg Foundation.

——. 2001. *Swedenborg's Dream Diary*. Edited by Lars Bergquist and translated by Anders Hallengren. West Chester, Pa.: Swedenborg Foundation.

Tafel, R. L. 1877. *Documents Concerning the Life and Character of Emanuel Swedenborg*. Vol. 2, parts 1 and 2. London: Swedenborg Society.

Trepp, A.–C, and Hartmut Lehmann, eds. 2001. *Antike Weisheit und kulturelle Praxis: Hermetismus in de Frühen Neuzeit*. Göttingen: Vandenhoeck & Ruprecht.

Vaihinger, Hans. 1881. *Commentar zu Kants Kritik der reinen Vernunft*, vol. I. Stuttgart: W. Spemann.

———. 1892. *Commentar zu Kants Kritik der reinen Vernunft*, vol. II. Stuttgart, Berlin, Leipzig: Union Deutsche Verlagsgesellschaft.

Versluis, Arthur. 1999. *Wisdom's Children: A Christian Esoteric Tradition.* Albany: State University of New York Press.

———. 2000. *Wisdom's Book: The Sophia Anthology.* St. Paul, Minn.: Paragon House.

———. 2001. *The Esoteric Origins of the American Renaissance.* Oxford: Oxford University Press.

Wilkinson, Lynn R. 1996. *The Dream of an Absolute Language: Emanuel Swedenborg and French Literary Culture.* Albany: State University of New York Press.

Williams, Arnold. 1948. *The Common Expositor: An Account of the Commentaries on Genesis, 1527–1633.* Chapel Hill, N.C.: University of North Carolina Press.

Williams-Hogan, Jane. 1998. "The Place of Emanuel Swedenborg in Modern Western Esotericism." In *Western Esotericism and the Science of Religion: Selected Papers presented at the 17th Congress of the International Association for the History of Religion, Mexico City 1995*, edited by Antoine Faivre and Wouter J. Hanegraaff. Louvain: Peeters. 201–252.

———. 2000. "Emanuel Swedenborg and the Jewish Kabbalah: Organic or Syncretic Relationship?" Paper presented at the symposium "Western Esotericism and Jewish Mysticism," 18th Quinquennial Congress of the International Association for the History of Religions, Durban, South Africa, August 5–12, 2000.

Woofenden, William Ross. 1992. "Doctrinal Patterns in *Arcana Coelestia.*" *Studia Swedenborgiana* 7:4.

———. 2002. *Swedenborg Explorer's Guidebook: A Research Manual for Inquiring New Readers, Seekers of Spiritual Ideas, and Writers of Swedenborgian Treatises.* 2nd ed. West Chester, Pa.: Swedenborg Foundation.

Wörner, Karl H. 1970. "Musik zwischen Theologie und Weltanschaaung." In *Die Musik in der Geistesgeschichte: Studien zur*

Situation der Jahre um 1910, edited by Karl H. Wörner. Bonn: Bouvier & Co.

Wunsch, William F. 1929. *The World within the Bible: A Handbook to Swedenborg's "Arcana Coelestia."* New York: The New-Church Press., repr. Kessinger publ. n.d.

Zimmermann, Rolf Christian. 1969–1979. *Das Weltbild des jungen Goethe.* 2 vols. München: Wilhelm Fink.

———. 1979. "Goethes Verhältnis zur Naturmystik am Beispiel seiner Farbenlehre." In *Epochen der Naturmystik: Hermetische Tradition im wissenschaftlichen Fortschritt*, edited by Antoine Faivre and Rolf Christian Zimmermann. Berlin: Erich Schmidt. 333–363.

❦ INDEX OF PERSONS ❧

Ernesti, Johann August, xviii, 60–65, 99, 129 (n. 91–92, 94–96)
Fabry, Jacques, 127 (n. 83)
Faivre, Antoine, xv, 118 (n. 6, 11), 119 (n. 13), 130 (n. 98), 133 (n. 116)
Feder, Georg Heinrich, 102, 138 (n. 163)
Fichte, Johann Gottlieb, 135 (n. 136)
Fischer, Kuno, 134 (n. 135), 137 (n. 150), 138 (n. 156), 140 (n. 176)
Florschütz, Gottlieb, 135 (n. 135)
Foucault, Michel, 106, 140 (n. 175)
Frederick the Great, 68
Fricker, Johann Ludwig, 70, 83–84, 128 (n. 85), 134 (n. 124)

Gaier, Ulrich, 111, 140 (n. 181)
Geier, Manfred, 136 (n. 145)
Goethe, Johann Wolfgang von, 59, 111–113, 117 (n. 1), 140 (n. 180)
Goya, Francisco, 140 (n. 174)
Gratzer, Wolfgang, 141 (n. 187)
Griffero, Tonino, 133 (n. 117), 135 (n. 135)

Hahn, Philipp Matthäus, 127 (n. 85)
Halldin, J.D., 129 (n. 89)
Hamann, Johann Georg, 89, 109, 136 (n. 143), 140 (n. 176)
Hanegraaff, Wouter J., ii, iv, x, xiii–xiv, 10, 44, 47, 53, 117 (n. 2, 4), 118
    (n. 6, 8, 10), 119 (n. 12), 124 (n. 53), 127 (n. 74), 135 (n. 136),
    141 (n 188)
Hartknoch, Johann Friedrich, 128 (n. 86)
Hartley, Thomas, 61
Hartmann, Israel, 81, 84, 128 (n. 85), 134 (n. 133)
Hasencamp, Rector, 81–82
Hecht, Koppel, 67
Hegel, Georg Wilhelm Friedrich, 135 (n. 136)
Heinrichs, Michael, 111, 134 (n. 135)
Helmont, Franciscus Mercurius van, xxi
Henck, Herbert, 84
Henke, Pastor, 81
Herder, Johann Gottfried, viii, 87, 89, 101, 138 (n. 157)
Herschel, William, 104

✦ INDEX OF SUBJECTS ✦

❦ AUTHOR BIOGRAPHY ❧

SINCE 1999 WOUTER J. HANEGRAAFF HAS BEEN PROFESSOR OF HISTORY of Hermetic Philosophy and Related Currents at the University of Amsterdam. From 2002–2006 he was president of the Dutch Society for the Study of Religion, and, since 2005, is president of the European Society for the Study of Western Esotericism. He was elected member of the Royal Dutch Academy of Sciences (KNAW) in 2006.

In addition to his acclaimed book *New Age Religion and Western Culture: Esotericism in the Mirror of Secular Thought* (Brill 1996/SUNY Press 1998), Hanegraaff with Ruud M. Bouthoorn has published a study titled *Lodovico Lazzarelli (1447–1500): The Hermetic Writings and Related Documents* (Arizona Center for Medieval and Renaissance Studies 2005), and edited a number of books in the study of religion and Western esotericism. In 2005 Hanegraaff edited the *Dictionary of Gnosis and Western Esotericism* (Brill) in collaboration with Antoine Faivre, Roelof van den Broek and Jean-Pierre Brach. He has served as co-editor of *Aries: Journal for the Study of Western Esotericism*, and also as editor-in-chief of the associated Aries Book Series. He has also served on the editorial board of the journals *Religion*, *Numen*, *Religion Compass*, and *Esoterica*, and on the advisory board of *Journal of Contemporary Religion* and *Nova Religio*.